★ ★ ★ *The Ultimate* ★ ★ ★

BURGER
BOOK

Text and recipes: Sabine Durdel-Hoffmann, Elke Eßmann, Brigitte Lotz

Advice: Burkhard Schröger

Picture credits: TLC Fotostudio (recipe photos); Fotolia.com: © ivanbaranov (Illustrations), © SP-PIC (wooden background)

The Ultimate

BURGER

BOOK

With and without meat

CONTENT

INTRODUCTION 6

All about burgers

BURGER BUNS 14

SIDE DISHES 16

SALADS 18

DIPS & SAUCES 20

Burger recipes

BEEF & VEAL 24

PORK 54

LAMB & GAME 70

POULTRY 86

FISH & SEAFOOD 102

VEGGIES 112

RECIPE INDEX 128

INTRODUCTION

When it comes to sheer popularity, nothing in the world beats the traditional burger, prepared the traditional American way. Only the best ingredients are used in the preparation, and the sum of its ingredients makes it irresistible. This icon of pleasure is available in a mind-blowing range of flavours and varieties – it's the perfect meal for gourmets of all ages!

Traditional accompaniments such as home-made fries, wedges or slaw are the perfect enhancement of this already perfect culinary delight. Tasty home-made burgers buns, ketchup, sauces and dips are the perfect finishing touches to the taste experience.

Anyone who has ever had the pleasure of dining at a good American burger restaurant, perhaps at Shake Shack, P. J. Clarke's or Bill's Bar and Burger in New York, and enjoying a freshly prepared burger prepared with consummate skill and passion knows just what a culinary treat it is. And there are almost as many stories about how it came to be as there are recipes for making it. Almost everyone believes that Hamburg, Germany's gateway to the world, is the original home of this meat patty, which is grilled, fried or barbecued and served in a roll or bun. In the 18th century, many Europeans departed from Hamburg to spend weeks at sea en route to a new home. They took with them a particular Hamburg speciality as fortification and to have something for their trip: a round bread roll that was filled with a slice of roast beef or seasoned, fried minced beef and with sauce. It filled them up, left them feeling full for some time, and was easy to eat in the hand. And even then, it tasted really good.

this also came from America, when a number of restaurant chains standardised its preparation and sale in the 1940s and 1950s. However, connoisseurs have long since come to terms with the origins, and know that a freshly prepared hamburger made with the best and freshest ingredients can be a gustatory revelation: the combination of grilled, seasoned meat, crispy-fresh vegetables and aromatic sauces, side dishes and dips is simply delicious. And there are so many different combinations that interesting new varieties are constantly being served up.

Restaurants and gourmets have long since taken up the American tradition of the skilfully prepared burger again, and create highly imaginative taste sensations that delight burger-lovers of all ages and classes. When it comes to the various recipes, it is impossible to deny the American roots, although they have long since spread themselves far and wide, and even

It is believed that beef was shipped to America, again from Hamburg harbour, as there was a serious lack of it in the "New World", which did not yet have any of the vast herds of cattle for which it is now famous. The English (or American) word "hamburger" originally referred to lean minced beef. No one knows exactly when which particular American restaurant or kiosk owner first thought up the hamburger that we know today. It might have been elegant "Delmonico's" in New York, Charlie Nagreen, Fletcher Davies, the Menches Brothers in Erie County, Louis Lunch in New Haven or any of numerous others. In fact, it is most likely that the burger as we know it actually came into being in several different places at the same time.

What is certain, though, is that the burger was extremely popular in America at the beginning of the 20th century. Originally, the hamburger was anything but a rather questionable form of fast food. The reasons for its reputation as

award-winning chefs the world over are pleased to serve up their variations of this success. It's undeniable: wherever it came from, the hamburger is more popular today than ever before.
Enjoy!

PREPARATION & INGREDIENTS

What makes a good burger?

First of all, there are "hamburgers" and there are "cheeseburgers". As the name implies, a cheeseburger is a burger to which a layer of cheese (or several layers, according to taste) have been added. We haven't made too much distinction in the following. Ultimately, it is up to the connoisseur to decide whether he wants cheese on his burger, how much of it and what kind it should be. You will find a basic recipe for the "classic" hamburger on page 26.

As a general rule, a hamburger can consist of several different variable components:

- meat or vegetarian ingredients for the **"patties"** (such as beef, pork, lamb, poultry, fish and seafood, bulgur or tofu)
- bread rolls or **buns** (for instance, wheat, rye, multigrain or ciabatta, brioches or all kinds of flat breads)

And for the **toppings:**

- salad, vegetables, fruit
- cheese (for instance blue cheese, brie, camembert, cheddar, feta, Gouda, Gruyère, halloumi, manchego, mozzarella, provolone, Taleggio, goat's cheese)
- dressing, marinade, pesto, tapenade, mayonnaise, mustard, ketchup, chutney, relish etc.
- herbs and spices

Making your own tasty burger has nothing to do with magic, even if the ingredients and artistic arrangements that you will often find in the burger restaurants would encourage you to think so. The utensils as well as the ingredients will already be found in most households. However, a little basic knowledge of the preparation as it is provided on the following pages of this book will certainly ensure that your efforts are a success.

The preparation is easy with our "modular system", and also opens up an endless variety of possible combinations. And you'll soon see that it's just as easy to produce your own creative combinations.

The grill

Whether a charcoal, gas or electric grill or barbecue, open or closed grill, ceramic or stainless steel grill: (almost) everyone has their own version at home. Basically, burgers can be cooked on almost any grill, and also in ridged or cast iron pans or skillets. For instance, you can fry the burger on both sides in a pan, then put in a pre-heated oven at 180 °C (Gas Mark 4) for 20-25 minutes to finish (depending on the ingredients and your preferred level of doneness).

Whether you use charcoal or briquettes on the grill is up to you. Charcoal glows sooner, but although briquettes take longer to get there, they glow for longer.

We prepared our recipes on a traditional charcoal grill with charcoal (not briquettes).

- As patties are smaller and flatter, they are ideal for **quick, direct grilling** over the charcoal. They heat up quickly, which creates a crispy outside, and they remain tender as they cook on the inside.
- **Charcoal** gives grilled burgers the unique smoky-roasted flavour that makes them so irresistible.
- And last, but by no means least: grilling the traditional way creates a unique atmosphere.

The accessories

To grill patties, you basically need the same utensils as for grilling other foods. However, it is a good idea to have some of them in duplicate.

- Barbecue or grill, charcoal, barbecue lighter
- Burger press. This is where opinions differ, but people who absolutely insist on having patties all the same size should opt for a press. But that's not to say it's essential ...
- Barbecue gloves, apron, paper towels for protection and for cleaning
- Grill brush with wire bristle to remove all traces of rust from the rack before cooking and prevent the burgers from sticking to it, or dirt particles from sticking to the burgers
- Tongs for rearranging the charcoal
- Several turners for the different kinds of foods

- Side table to put the cooked food on and rest your utensils on
- Several plates, again for the cooked food, and for the utensils when you have used them
- Heatproof oil (vegetable oil) and brushed for oiling the rack
- Brushes for brushing the food during cooking
- Any spices, glazes and other ingredients that you wish to brush over the burgers while you are cooking them

The ingredients

There are a few points that you need to observe so you can be sure that your burgers are far superior in flavour and consistency to the ready-made products that can bought from fast-food chains, for instance. The most important thing is the quality of your ingredients.

MEAT

The classic burger was made with minced beef, usually cooked medium, but the list of options has been greatly extended, and today even includes exotic rarities such as ostrich. Whether you used minced or whole meat for the patties, it should always contain a certain amount of fat (about 18–20 percent), as this is what keeps it juicy and tender during cooking. Furthermore, it is the fat that gives meat its "meaty" flavour, and it is also the carrier for other flavours. It is easy to be sure of the origin and quality of organic meat, which you can obtain from farm shops, most supermarkets and high-street butchers. Minced meat in particular should be absolutely fresh, kept cool during transportation and until you are ready to use it, then used as quickly as possible after purchase to prevent bacteria from developing. Ask your trusted butcher to grind your meat freshly so you can be absolutely sure of it. Also ask him not to squeeze the minced meat when wrapping it up; you will then find it easier to combine it with the other ingredients when preparing the burgers, and the burgers will not be too tough later on. It is best if the minced meat is cooked all the way through.

You can also combine different kinds of meat, such as lamb and beef, pork and lamb, veal and beef, or beef and pork. The addition of an egg and breadcrumbs will make the mixture looser, but is not to everyone's taste. You can also use just one egg, instead of the two given in the recipes. If the mixture is too wet, add some more breadcrumbs – you'll find it's very much a matter of

feeling. Mie de pain (fine white breadcrumbs without crusts) has a finer texture.

You can use just about any part of an animal to make burgers. You can use chicken breast fillets or other whole (that is, unminced) pieces of tender meat instead of minced meat, and in fact it's better that way if you are making your burgers with fish. Whether you prefer lean fillet, and possibly even exclusive wagyu beef, is a matter of taste – and price. You can marinate the meat and fish before using it.

Some pieces are better than others:

Beef

The meat should be well hung, a rich red in colour and finely marbled with fat. Flank, entrecôte, chuck steak or neck are good choices. Basically, you can use whatever you like, but the leaner the meat is, the more fat there should be in the other ingredients the patties.

Veal

Veal is pale pink and more finely textured. As it has a delicate flavour, it should be seasoned with care. Shoulder and haunch are good choices for burgers.

Pork

The flesh should ideally be a fresh pink and evenly marbled. Back, belly, fore or hind leg – basically, it all depends on how much fat you like in your burgers.

Lamb

Fresh lamb should be a velvety red with white fat. Try shoulder or back. Lamb has a very strong taste, and can cope with a good quantity of seasoning or very strong spices and herbs.

Game

The choice is yours: venison, wild boar, rabbit or other type of game. Ask your butcher. Whichever you choose, all are strong in flavour, and this should be taken into account when barbecuing burgers.

Poultry

Chicken, turkey, duck or goose – the tender flesh of the breast fillets (either whole or minced by your butcher) is the most popular. As a general rule, use poultry quickly, and do not use any of the equipment for other tasks without first washing it thoroughly.

Fish

You can, of course, grind fish and seafood if you so desire. Remember, though, that burgers made with minced fish or seafood will easily fall apart. It is a good idea to barbecue or grill fish or fish fillets and seafood either whole items or as fillets. Choose types with a high fat content (salmon, halibut, swordfish, bass or tuna) so the burger doesn't end up too dry, and seafood (for example squid, mussels, oysters and scallops) without the shells, of course. All are excellent if you marinate them before cooking.

ROLLS AND BUNS

The buns not only provide the right setting, but they are more than just a "side", and therefore have to perform a small miracle: they need to be soft enough so that the contents don't fall out when you bite into them and end up on the floor or, worse, on your lap.

They should also be dense enough not to absorb too much liquid so they turn soggy.

As well as the classic, the "white burger bun" (with or without sesame seeds, recipe on page 15), you can use any kind of roll or bun as long as it meets the above requirements. Those who prefer something a little heartier will enjoy a rye bun (recipe on page 15), while diners with more Mediterranean preferences might want to opt for ciabatta (recipe on page 15).

You can also use bought rolls or buns; most supermarkets and bakers offer a wide selection of good quality alternatives. You could also try brioches or hearty sourdough rolls, Indian naan bread, Turkish flatbreads or just thick slices ("doorsteps") of plain white bread – the only limits are your own imagination! However, whichever type you choose, it's better if it's not too crispy.

A little hint to help prevent the burger contents from slipping around: skewer them with a cocktail stick before serving.

TOPPINGS, DRESSINGS, SEASONING & MORE

You, and you alone, decide what you're going to have on your burger, and the possibilities are almost endless. You can also add additional flavour depending on how you prepare the various ingredients. **Spices** can be dry-fried, **vegetables grilled, barbecued or roasted, onions fried or caramelised** – and that's just the start. You can also choose from many different types of mustard, ketchup and mayonnaise.

Cheese should melt and develop its aromas but without sliding off the burger, which makes some varieties more suitable than others. Firm cheese-based products are another option, light soured cream and herb quark yet more.

You will find information on meat density, cooking times and suitable herbs and spices in the introductions to the various chapters.

On pages 15 to 23 are a few basic recipes that are varied in our recipe suggestions.

But be as creative as you can – to quote so many of the burger menus that you will find all over the world: **build your own burger!**

Tips & tricks

There are a few things you need to take to heart in order to enjoy tasty burgers:

- If you use a lighter or lighter fluid, make sure it burns off completely so it doesn't contaminate the food you are cooking.
- Do not put the food on the rack while the charcoal is still throwing flames – not only is this dangerous to the people standing around, but they will also burn the meat and render it inedible.
- Brush the grid with heat-proof vegetable oil to prevent the patties from sticking.
- Use the practical "building block" system: do you have a particular favourite in the beef section, but want to try it with a topping from the pork section you prefer – or even adapt it slightly? You decide which buns you want to combine with which patties and toppings.
- Prepare more lavish toppings before you start to cook and keep them warm or cool, or else wrap the prepared burgers in clingfilm and chill while you prepare the toppings. You can make excellent use of soaking and marinating times for your necessary preparations!
- If a mixture is rather loose (perhaps if you haven't quite developed the knack for using breadcrumbs and eggs), and you are concerned about it disintegrating while cooking on the grill, wrap it in clingfilm and chill before cooking, and the patty will hold its shape better.
- If possible, only turn the patties once so they don't dry out or crumble. Always use a spatula for turning, and always be patient! If you leave the patty for long enough, it will easily loosen from the rack by itself.
- Do not press down on the patties with the spatula while they are cooking, or the meat will dry out.
- Cook fish in aluminium foil or a fish basket so it doesn't crumble.
- Season sparingly, since the flavours don't start to develop properly until the food heats up.

BURGER BUNS

WHEAT BUNS

CIABATTA BUNS

RYE BUNS

WHEAT BUNS

Makes 10–12 buns, preparation time:
approx. 20 minutes (plus standing, rising
and baking time)
Per bun approx.:
211 kcal/883 kJ, 7 g P, 7 g F, 31 g CH

INGREDIENTS
approx. 200 ml milk
50 g butter
500 g wheat flour (type 405)
50 g yeast
1 egg
1 tsp salt
pinch of sugar
1 egg yolk
sesame seeds to sprinkle

1| Heat the milk and butter in a small
saucepan without boiling. Meanwhile,
put the flour in a bowl and make a well
in the middle. Crumble in the yeast.

2| Gradually pour the warm liquid over
the yeast, stirring it with the dough
hook of an electric hand mixer at the
same time (low speed) to make a pre-
dough. Cover the bowl with a clean tea
towel and leave the dough in a warm
place for about 10 minutes to rise.

3| Add the egg, salt and sugar to the pre-
dough and stir until the dough starts to
froth and comes away from the side of
the bowl. Cover the bowl again and
return the dough to the warm place for
about 25 minutes to rise.

4| Pre-heat the oven to 200 °C (Gas
Mark 6, fan oven 180 °C). Knead the
dough thoroughly with floured hands,
and divide into 12 portions. Shape each
piece into a ball and place on a baking
sheet lined with baking parchment.
Cover, and leave to stand for 10 minutes. Then press down lightly on them.
Be sure to leave plenty of space
between the buns, because they will
rise as they bake.

5| Brush the buns with whisked egg yolk,
and sprinkle with the sesame seeds if
desired. Bake in the pre-heated oven
for 20 minutes, making sure they do
not get too dark and crispy.

Eat while still fresh.

RYE BUNS

Makes 10–12 buns, preparation time:
approx. 20 minutes (plus standing, rising
and baking time)
Per bun approx.:
183 kcal/766 kJ, 6 g P, 5 g F, 28 g CH

INGREDIENTS
200 ml milk
50 g butter
300 g finely-grained rye
200 g wheat flour (type 550)
1 cube of yeast (50 g)
1 egg, 1 tsp salt
1 tbsp sugar beet syrup or stewed apple

1| Heat the milk and butter in a small
saucepan without boiling. Meanwhile,
put the flours in a bowl and combine.
Make a well in the middle and crumble
in the yeast.

2| Gradually pour the warm liquid over
the yeast, stirring it with the dough
hook of an electric hand mixer at the
same time (low speed) to make a pre-
dough. Cover the bowl with a clean tea
towel and leave the dough in a warm
place for about 10 minutes to rise.

3| Add the egg, salt and syrup to the pre-
dough and stir until the dough starts to
froth and comes away from the side of
the bowl. Cover the bowl again and
return the dough to the warm place for
about 25 minutes to rise.

4| Pre-heat the oven to 200 °C (Gas
Mark 6, fan oven 180 °C). Knead the
dough thoroughly with floured hands,
and divide into 12 portions. Shape each
piece into a ball and place on a baking
tray lined with baking parchment.
Cover, and leave to stand for 10 minutes. Then press down lightly on them.
Be sure to leave plenty of space
between the buns, because they will
rise as they bake.

5| Bake in the pre-heated oven for
20 minutes. Put a dish of water in the
oven with the buns and sprinkle them
several times with water so they don't
get too crispy - they should stay quiet
soft.

Eat while still fresh.

CIABATTA BUNS

Makes 10–12 buns, preparation time:
approx. 20 minutes (plus standing, rising
and baking time)
Per bun approx.:
161 kcal/674 kJ, 5 g P, 3 g F, 30 g CH

INGREDIENTS
500 g wheat flour (type 550) plus
    flour to dust
25 g yeast
1 level tbsp salt
25 ml olive oil

1| Sift the flour into a bowl and make a
well in the middle. Crumble in the
yeast, and gradually add 300 ml of
water to make a pre-dough (using the
dough hook of a mixer). Cover the bowl
with a clean tea towel and leave in a
warm place for about 20 minutes for
the dough to rise.

2| Add the salt and oil to the pre-dough
and knead until smooth. The dough
should be very moist. Cover again, and
leave at room temperature for at least
12 hours to rise - ideally overnight. This
will make the dough very airy with
large pores.

3| Dust the worktop and dough gener-
ously with flour. Use a dough scraper to
carefully divide the dough, press down
gently and fold - the idea is to retain
the airiness. Cover again, and leave for
another hour. Pre-heat the oven to
220 °C (Gas Mark 7, fan oven 200 °C).

4| Carefully divide the dough into 12 seg-
ments, and shape them into ciabatta
buns. Place on a baking tray lined with
baking parchment, leaving plenty of
space between the buns. Bake on the
bottom runner for about 30 minutes.
Sprinkle frequently with water while
baking so the buns stay nice and moist.

Eat while still fresh.

SIDE DISHES

HOME-MADE FRIES

For 4 portions, preparation time:
approx. 15 minutes (plus frying time)
Per portion approx.:
329 kcal/1377 kJ, 3 g P, 28 g F, 84 g CH

INGREDIENTS
600 g oil for deep-frying
6 large potatoes
salt

1| Pre-heat the deep-fryer and pour in the oil.

2| Peel and wash the potatoes and cut into thick chips. Pat dry with kitchen paper so they are as dry as possible. Once the deep-fryer has reached 160 °C, put the potatoes in the hot oil for 10 minutes.

3| Lift out the potatoes and put in a large sieve lined with paper towels to drain.

4| Increase the temperature of the deep-fryer to 180 °C and fry the pre-cooked potatoes in the hot oil for a further 5 minutes until golden and crispy. Place on kitchen paper to dry, then put in a bowl and sprinkle with salt according to taste.

WEDGES

For 4 portions, preparation time:
approx. 15 minutes (plus cooking time)
Per portion approx.:
250 kcal/1046 kJ, 4 g P, 9 g F, 29 g CH

INGREDIENTS
800 g potatoes
4 tbsp vegetable oil
1 tsp paprika powder
salt

1| Pre-heat the oven to 200 °C (Gas Mark 6, fan oven 180 °C).

2| Wash the potatoes well, then dry them and cut into long wedges. Combine in a bowl with the oil, ground paprika and salt.

3| Line a baking sheet with baking parchment and arrange the potato wedges on it. Bake in the oven for 30–40 minutes.

NACHOS

For 4 portions, preparation time:
approx.: 15 minutes (plus standing and baking time)
Per portion approx.:
278 kcal/1163 kJ, 1 g P, 8 g F, 46 g CH

INGREDIENTS
250 g maize meal
½ tsp salt
sunflower oil for frying
sweet paprika powder to sprinkle

1| Sift the maize meal into a bowl and gradually pour in 250 ml lukewarm water. Knead slowly to make a smooth dough, then leave it to rest for 5-7 minutes. Knead again with the salt.

2| Put the dough on one piece of baking parchment and cover with another one, then roll out with a rolling pin until very thin (2 mm). Cut out slices of any diameter.

3| Heat the oil in a non-stick pan and fry the dough circles in batches over a medium heat for half a minute on each side.

4| Leave to cool, then cut into large triangles. Deep fry or bake in a pre-heated oven until crispy, and season to taste.

SALADS

CAESAR'S SALAD

For 4 portions, preparation time:
approx. 20 minutes
Per portion approx.:
761 kcal/3184 kJ, 14 g P, 73 g F, 3 g CH

INGREDIENTS
2 thick slices white bread
200 ml olive oil plus a little extra for
    roasting
2 small romaine lettuces
1 avocado
2 tbsp lemon juice
1 garlic clove
4 anchovies
1 egg yolk
1 tbsp Worcester sauce
salt
sugar
100 g Parmesan

1| Cut the crusts of the slices of bread and
dice the bread. Heat a little olive oil in a
non-stick pan and fry the bread cubes
until golden. Set aside.

2| Trim, wash and spin dry the lettuces
and shred the leaves with your fingers.
Halve the avocado. Remove the stone
and scoop the flesh out of the shells.
Dice the flesh and sprinkle with a little
lemon juice.

3| Peel and finely chop the garlic, and
chop the anchovies. Stir together the
egg yolk and the remainder of the
lemon juice. Add the olive oil in drop,
then in a thin stream, and stir well.
Combine with the Worcester sauce and
seasoning until creamy, and check
whether more seasoning is required.

4| Combine the salad and the dressing.
Sprinkle over the croutons and grate
over the Parmesan in rough flakes.

COLE SLAW

For 4 portions, preparation time:
approx. 30 minutes (plus standing time)
Per portion approx.:
167 kcal/699 kJ, 6 g P, 8 g F, 16 g CH

INGREDIENTS
1 small white cabbage
2-3 small carrots
2 shallots
150 g plain yoghurt
50 g mayonnaise
juice of ½ lemon
1 tbsp cider vinegar
1 tbsp sugar
salt
freshly ground pepper

1| Remove the outer leaves of the cab-
bage. Cut the cabbage into large
pieces, then thinly slice the leaves.
Trim, peel and grate the carrots. Peel
and dice the shallots.

2| Combine the remainder of the ingredi-
ents to make a salad cream, and combine with the vegetables. The salad
should not be too dry. Place in the
refrigerator and leave for 1 hour.

3| Remove the salad from the fridge
about 15 minutes before serving so it is
not too cold.

WILD GARDEN HERB SALAD

For 4 portions, preparation time:
approx. 15 minutes
Per portion approx.:
138 kcal/577 kJ, 2 g P, 10 g F, 3 g CH

INGREDIENTS
2 cherry tomatoes
1 small cucumber
120 g rocket
40 g dandelion leaves
20 g sorrel
3 large wild garlic leaves
1 finely chopped shallot
½ tsp Dijon mustard
3 tbsp white balsamic vinegar
4 tbsp pumpkin seed oil
pinch of sugar
salt
freshly ground pepper

1| Wash and quarter the cherry tomatoes.
Peel the cucumber with a vegetable
peeler and cut into slices. Trim or wash
and shake dry the salad leaves and
herbs, then shred them.

2| Combine the remainder
of the ingredients to
make a dressing, then
check the seasoning
and combine with the
salad.

**Choose salad leaves and
herbs of the season that
you like.**

DEEP-FRIED ONION RINGS

For 4 portions, preparation time:
approx. 40 minutes
Per portion approx.:
260 kcal/1087 kJ, 8 g P, 10 g F, 28 g CH

INGREDIENTS
oil for deep-frying
2 Spanish onions
150 g wheat flour
2 eggs
salt
70 ml beer

1| Heat the oil in a large saucepan or
deep-fat fryer (to about 180 °C).

2| Peel the onions and cut into thick rings.
Stir together all the remaining ingredients to make a batter. Dip the onion
rings in the batter and deep-fry until
golden. Place on kitchen paper to drain.

WILD GARDEN HERB SALAD

DIPS & SAUCES

MAYONNAISE

For 4 portions, preparation time:
approx. 10 minutes
Per portion approx.:
51 kcal/213 kJ, 2 g P, 9 g F, 1 g CH

INGREDIENTS
1 egg yolk
1 tbsp lemon juice
1 tbsp mustard
pinch of salt
pinch of freshly ground pepper
pinch of sugar
125 ml neutral oil
other ingredients to taste

Stir together all the ingredients except the oil in a bowl. Add the oil first in drops, then in a thin stream, stirring continuously until the mayonnaise takes on a smooth, fine, creamy consistency.

You can flavour this basic mayonnaise to suit your menu and tastes with spices, chopped herbs, ground herbs, ketchup, chopped egg, grated lemon ring and juice – and much more.

AIOLI

For 4 portions, preparation time:
approx. 10 minutes
Per portion approx.:
624 kcal/2611 kJ, 2 g P, 66 g F, 2 g CH

INGREDIENTS
2 egg yolks
1 tbsp lemon juice
5 garlic cloves
260 ml olive oil
salt
freshly ground pepper

Stir together the egg yolks and lemon juice, then peel the garlic cloves and crush into the egg yolk mixture. Stir in the olive oil in drops until you have a mayonnaise. Season according to taste.

SOUR CREAM

For 4 portions, preparation time:
approx. 10 minutes
Per portion approx.:
47 kcal/197 kJ, 5 g P, 2 g F, 3 g CH

INGREDIENTS
½ bunch curly-leafed parsley
125 g low-fat quark
125 g plain yoghurt
1 tbsp sliced chives
½ finely chopped onion
dash of lemon juice
salt
freshly ground pepper

Wash and shake dry the parsley and chop the leaves very finely. Combine well with the other ingredients, then checking the seasoning and chill.

SOUR CREAM

GUACAMOLE

GUACAMOLE

For 4 portions, preparation time:
approx. 10 minutes
Per portion approx.:
262 kcal/1096 kJ, 127 g P, 0 g F, 29 g CH

INGREDIENTS
2 avocados
8 coriander stalks
1 small onion, finely chopped
1 small red chilli, deseeded and finely chopped
salt, freshly ground pepper

1| Halve the avocados. Remove the stones and set them aside. Scoop the flesh out of the shells with a spoon and mash in a bowl with a fork. Wash and shake dry the coriander. Pluck off the leaves and chop very finely.

2| Combine all the ingredients and check the seasoning. Put the avocado stones back in with the purée, as they will help to retain its bright green colour.

KETCHUP

For 4 portions, preparation time:
approx. 20 minutes
Per portion approx.:
127 kcal/531 kJ, 6 g P, 0 g F, 29 g CH

INGREDIENTS
4 apples, 4 finely chopped onions
400 g tomato purée
1 tbsp curry powder
pinch of salt, pinch of cinnamon
1 tbsp sugar beet syrup
100 ml cider vinegar

1| Peel and quarter the apples and cut out the cores. Chop into very small pieces.

2| Put all the ingredients in a sauce with a little water (to your preferred consistency). Simmer until soft, then purée very finely. Pour the ketchup into clean bottles, then seal well and keep in a cool place.

BBQ SAUCE

Makes 600 ml, preparation time:
approx. 20 minutes (plus standing and cooking time)
Per portion approx.
129 kcal/540 kJ, 3 g P, 1 g F, 17 g CH

INGREDIENTS
1 smoked chipotle pepper
75 ml cider vinegar
750 g vine tomatoes
1 chopped Spanish onion
2 chopped garlic cloves
50 g brown sugar
1 tbsp sugar beet syrup
1 tbsp hot mustard
1 tsp salt
1 tsp freshly ground pepper
1 tsp chilli powder
pinch of ground cumin seed

1| Put the chilli in a small bowl and pour over a little vinegar. Cover, and leave to stand at room temperature for 1 day, then chop. Cut a cross in the tomatoes, then pour over boiling water and skin. Remove the stalks and chop the flesh. Take the chilli out of the vinegar and chop.

2| Put the chilli, tomatoes, onion and garlic in a saucepan with the remainder of the vinegar and bring to the boil. Stir in the sugar, sugar beet syrup, mustard, salt, pepper, ground chilli and ground cumin seed and simmer, stirring, for about 30 minutes. Then pass through a fine sieve into a clean saucepan and boil until thick.

BEEF & VEAL

It is a good idea to cook patties made of minced beef and veal, about 2 cm thick, over a medium to high heat for a total of about 3-4 minutes on each side. Of course, the exact time depends on the food you are cooking, the barbecue or grill and - not least - your personal taste.

The meat harmonises well with spices and herbs such as chilli, garlic, oregano, paprika, parsley, rosemary, sage or thyme.

HAMBURGERS

FOR 4 PORTIONS
PREPARATION TIME: APPROX. 30 MINUTES

Per portion approx.:
790 kcal/3305 kJ
57 g P   44 g F   53 g CH

BUNS

4 sesame wheat buns (recipe on page 15)

PATTIES

Basics:
600 g minced beef
salt
freshly ground pepper

To bulk out and bind:
1 stale bread roll
approx. 120 ml lukewarm milk
1 finely chopped onion
2 eggs

Spices & flavouring:
3 tbsp finely chopped red pepper
pinch of chilli powder
1 tsp dried thyme
1 tsp dried rosemary

TOPPINGS

4 green lettuce leaves
2 pickled gherkins
4 tomatoes
4 slices Gouda
4 tsp ketchup (recipe on page 22)
4 tsp mayonnaise (recipe on page 20)

The basics for a classic hamburger patty are good meat, salt and - if desired - pepper; you don't really need anything else. A bread roll, onions and eggs will bulk out the patty and help to bind the ingredients; the quantities depend on your personal preference. You can also add spices and flavourings if you like.

1| Dice the bread roll and soak in the milk for 10 minutes, then squeeze out well. Put all the ingredients except the seasoning in a bowl, and combine well. Season to taste.

2| With damp hands, shape the mixture into 4 patties, then grill on each side for about 3-4 minutes. Halve the burger buns and toast the cut surfaces over the grill for a few moments.

3| To make the toppings, wash and shake dry the lettuce leaves. Thinly slice the gherkins. Wash the tomatoes, cut out the stalks and cut the flesh into thin slices.

4| Place 1 lettuce leaf, some gherkin slices, the patty, a slice of cheese and some tomato slices on the bottom halves of the buns. Spread with 1 teaspoon ketchup and 1 teaspoon mayonnaise, and top with the other half of the bun.

Goes with
CORN ON THE COB

Per portion approx.:
103 kcal/431 kJ
7 g P   29 g F   33 g CH

4 fresh corn on the cob, salt
125 g cold butter
4 garlic cloves
freshly ground pepper

Remove the leaves and threads from the corn on the cob and boil in salted water for about 15 minutes. Drain, and place on the grill for about 15 minutes, turning frequently. Cut the butter into pieces. Combine with the crushed garlic and seasoning, and spread over the corn on the cob.

DOUBLE-DOUBLE
CHEESEBURGERS

FOR 4 PORTIONS
PREPARATION TIME: APPROX. 30 MINUTES

Per portion approx.:
1061 kcal/4439 kJ
65 g P   86 g F   64 g CH

BUNS

4 sesame wheat buns (recipe on page 15)

PATTIES

1 stale bread roll
approx. 120 ml lukewarm milk
600 g minced beef
3 tbsp finely chopped red pepper
1 finely chopped onion
2 eggs
½ tsp chilli powder
1-2 tbsp Worcester sauce
1 tsp dried thyme
1 tsp dried rosemary
salt
freshly ground pepper

TOPPINGS

4 large green lettuce leaves
2 pickled gherkins
1 red onion
ketchup (recipe on page 22)
mayonnaise (recipe on page 20)
8 slices young Gouda
8 slices semi-mature Gouda

1| Dice the bread roll and soak in the milk for 10 minutes, then squeeze out well. Put all the ingredients except the seasoning in a bowl, and combine well. Season to taste.

2| With damp hands, shape the mixture into 4 patties, then grill on each side for about 3-4 minutes. Halve the burger buns and toast the cut surfaces over the grill for a few moments.

3| To make the toppings, wash and shake dry the lettuce leaves. Thinly slice the gherkins. Peel the onion and cut into thick slices.

4| If you like, put thick blobs of ketchup and mayonnaise on the bottom halves of the buns. Place 1 lettuce leaf on each. Top this with 1 slice each of the young Gouda and 1 of the semi-mature at an angle so that the differently-coloured corners of the cheese can be seen. Place 1 patty and another slice of the young and semi-mature cheese on top, again with the cheeses at an angle. Arrange the sliced gherkins on top, and garnish with the onion rings. Top with the remaining halves of the buns.

Serve with ketchup and mayonnaise.

BUFFALO RANCH BURGERS

FOR 4 PORTIONS
PREPARATION TIME: APPROX. 30 MINUTES

Per portion approx.:
839 kcal/3510 kJ
50 g P   50 g F   44 g CH

BUNS

4 rye buns (recipe on page 15)

PATTIES

1 stale bread roll
approx. 120 ml lukewarm milk
600 g minced beef (Black Angus or similar
    quality)
3 tsp finely chopped black olives
1 tbsp finely chopped onion
2 eggs
pinch of jalapeño chilli powder
1-2 tsp jerk seasoning (Jamaican BBQ
    seasoning)
salt
freshly ground pepper

TOPPINGS

1 small romaine lettuce
3 tbsp balsamic vinegar
2 tbsp olive oil
1 tbsp forest honey
1 tbsp pine kernels
salt
freshly ground pepper
4 thick slices of Gorgonzola

1| Dice the bread roll and soak in the milk for 10 minutes, then squeeze out well. Put all the ingredients for the patties except the seasoning in a bowl, and combine well. Season to taste.

2| With damp hands, shape the mixture into 4 patties, then grill on each side for about 3-4 minutes. Halve the burger buns and toast the cut surfaces over the grill for a few moments.

3| To make the toppings, wash the lettuce leaves and tear the leaves with your fingers. Stir together the balsamic vinegar, olive oil, forest honey, pine kernels, salt and pepper for the dressing, and arrange the salad. The salad should not be too wet.

4| Arrange the salad on the bottom halves of the buns. Place a patty and 1 slice of Gorgonzola on each. Grind some pepper over each burger and top with the remaining halves of the buns. Serve with BBQ sauce (recipe on page 23) and fried onion rings (recipe on page 19).

As a tasty alternative to the patty take a medium-rare rump steak.

Goes with
MARSALA MUSHROOMS

Per portion approx.:
126 kcal/527 kJ
2 g P   7 g F   1 g CH

olive oil for frying
1 finely chopped shallot
250 g brown button mushrooms
100 ml Marsala
20 g butter
salt and freshly ground pepper

Heat the olive oil in a pan and fry the shallot-dices over a medium heat until glassy. Trim the button mushrooms and wipe with a damp cloth, then slice. Add to the shallot-dices and increase the heat, shaking the pan from time to time. Continue cooking over a medium heat for a few more minutes, then pour over the Marsala. Reduce the liquid and add the butter to bind. Check the seasoning, and serve.

HOT HAMBURGERS

FOR 4 PORTIONS
PREPARATION TIME: APPROX. 25 MINUTES

Per portion approx.:
834 kcal/3490 kJ
45 g P   56 g F   35 g CH

BUNS

4 sesame wheat buns (recipe on page 15)

PATTIES

1 stale bread roll
approx. 120 ml lukewarm milk
600 g minced beef
3 tbsp finely chopped red pepper
1 finely chopped onion
2 tbsp roughly chopped flat-leafed parsley
2 eggs
½ tsp chilli powder
1 tsp dried thyme
salt
freshly ground pepper

TOPPINGS

8 iceberg lettuce leaves
120 g herb butter

1| Dice the bread roll and soak in the milk for 10 minutes, then squeeze out well. Put all the ingredients for the patties except the seasoning in a bowl, and combine well. Season to taste.

2| With damp hands, shape the mixture into 4 patties, then grill on each side for about 3-4 minutes. Halve the burger buns and toast the cut surfaces over the grill for a few moments.

3| To make the toppings, wash the lettuce and shake dry, then thinly slice the leaves. Spread the bottom half of the bun thinly with herb butter while still warm. Top with the sliced lettuce leaves. Place the patty on top, and put 1 thick slice of herb butter on the warm patty to melt before serving.

These burgers go well with thin fries and herb or lemon mayonnaise (basic mayonnaise recipe on page 20).

Goes with
PAPRIKA RELISH

Per portion approx.:
101 kcal/424 kJ
2 g P   7 g F   9 g CH

2 red peppers
1 finely chopped onion
2 tbsp oil
1 garlic clove
½ tsp paprika powder
4 tbsp white wine vinegar
salt
1 tbsp sugar
freshly ground pepper

Deseed and wash the pepper, then chop into small pieces. Sauté the diced onion in hot oil until glassy. Add the chopped peppers, garlic and paprika powder, and simmer for 4–5 minutes. Stir in about 8 tablespoons of water, the vinegar, salt and sugar and simmer for about 40 minutes to reduce until velvety and smooth. Season with salt and pepper. Purée if you want to. Allow to cool before serving.

MEDITERRANEAN
BURGERS

FOR 4 PORTIONS
PREPARATION TIME: APPROX. 30 MINUTES

Per portion approx.:
764 kcal/3197 kJ
49 g P   44 g F   42 g CH

BUNS

4 ciabatta buns (recipe on page 15)

PATTIES

1 stale bread roll
approx. 120 ml lukewarm milk
1 courgette
600 g minced beef
1 finely chopped onion
2 eggs
½ tsp paprika powder
1 tsp dried oregano
salt
freshly ground pepper

TOPPINGS

4 large green lettuce leaves
1 beef tomato
200 g feta cheese
4 tbsp BBQ sauce (recipe on page 23)
freshly ground pepper
12 Kalamata olives, pitted

1| Dice the bread roll and soak in the milk for 10 minutes, then squeeze out well. Wash and trim the courgette, then chop finely or grate. Put all the ingredients for the patties except the seasoning in a bowl, and combine well. Season to taste.

2| With damp hands, shape the mixture into 4 patties, then grill on each side for about 3-4 minutes. Halve the burger buns and toast the cut surfaces over the grill for a few moments.

3| To make the toppings, wash and shake dry the lettuce leaves. Wash the tomato and cut into 8 slices, discarding the stalk. Carefully cut the feta cheese into thin slices or small segments.

4| Spread the bottom halves of the buns with the BBQ sauce. Arrange the lettuce leaves, tomato slices and patties on top. Top with the feta cheese, and grind over some pepper. Garnish with olives. Place the tops of the buns on top, and serve with extra BBQ sauce.

MEXICAN BURGERS

FOR 4 PORTIONS
PREPARATION TIME: APPROX. 35 MINUTES

Per portion approx.:
834 kcal/3490 kJ
46 g P   48 g F   58 g CH

BUNS

4 wheat buns (recipe on page 15)

PATTIES

1 stale bread roll
approx. 120 ml lukewarm milk
100 g sweetcorn (can)
600 g minced beef
1 finely chopped onion
2 eggs
1 tbsp hot mustard
2 tbsp chopped coriander leaves
½ tsp paprika powder
salt
freshly ground pepper

TOPPINGS

1 ripe avocado
1 finely chopped shallot
1 finely chopped garlic clove
1 tbsp light soured cream
juice of ½ lemon
salt
freshly ground pepper
big pinch of cayenne pepper
4 large green lettuce leaves
2 tomatoes
1 onion

1| Dice the bread roll and soak in the milk for 10 minutes, then squeeze out well. Drain the sweetcorn. Put all the ingredients except the seasoning in a bowl, and combine well. Season to taste.

2| With damp hands, shape the mixture into 4 patties, then grill on each side for about 3-4 minutes. Halve the burger buns and toast the cut surfaces over the grill for a few moments.

3| To make the toppings, halve the avocado, then peel and remove the stone. Put the flesh of the avocado in a bowl and mash with a fork. Stir in the diced shallot, garlic, soured cream and lemon juice, then season with salt, pepper and cayenne pepper.

4| Wash and shake dry the lettuce leaves. Wash and slice the tomatoes, cutting out the stalk. Peel and thinly slice the onion. Put the lettuce leaves on the bottom halves of the buns. Place the patties on the leaves and brush with avocado cream. Arrange the tomato slices on top and garnish with onion rings. Top with the remaining halves of the buns.

CHANTERELLE
BURGERS

FOR 4 PORTIONS
PREPARATION TIME: APPROX. 30 MINUTES (PLUS COOKING TIME)

Per portion approx.:
821 kcal/3435 kJ
54 g P   49 g F   49 g CH

BUNS

4 wheat buns (recipe on page 15)

PATTIES

1 stale bread roll
approx. 120 ml lukewarm milk
3 tbsp pine kernels
600 g minced beef
3 tbsp pickled capers
1 tsp dried oregano
2 eggs
salt
freshly ground pepper

TOPPINGS

4 large oak leaf lettuce leaves
400 g chanterelles
4 spring onions
2 tbsp butter
salt
freshly ground pepper
4 tbsp chopped flat-leafed parsley
4 tsp BBQ sauce (recipe on page 23)
4 slices cheddar

1| Dice the bread roll and soak in the milk for 10 minutes, then squeeze out well. Finely chop the pine kernels. Put all the ingredients except the seasoning in a bowl, and combine well. Season to taste.

2| With damp hands, shape the mixture into 4 patties, then grill on each side for about 3-4 minutes. Halve the burger buns and toast the cut surfaces over the grill for a few moments.

3| To make the toppings, wash and shake dry the lettuce leaves. Trim the chanterelles and cut in half if necessary. Trim, wash and thinly slice the spring onions.

4| Melt the butter in a pan and sauté the mushrooms over a medium heat for about 10 minutes. Season with salt and pepper when cooked and stir in the parsley.

5| Drizzle 1 teaspoon of barbecue sauce over the bottom halves of the buns. Place a salad leaf and patty on each half. Arrange the chanterelles evenly over the top, and garnish with the spring onions. Finish with 1 slice of cheese. Top with the other halves of the buns, and secure each bun with a wooden cocktail stick.

BURGERS WITH BACON
AND RADISHES

FOR 4 PORTIONS
PREPARATION TIME: APPROX. 30 MINUTES

Per portion approx.:
664 kcal/2778 kJ
46 g P   38 g F   36 g CH

BUNS

4 rye buns (recipe on page 15)

PATTIES

1 stale bread roll
approx. 120 ml lukewarm milk
100 g smoked streaky bacon
600 g minced beef
1 finely chopped onion
2 eggs
1 tbsp hot mustard
2 tbsp sliced chives
salt
freshly ground pepper

TOPPINGS

4 large green lettuce leaves
1 bunch radishes
½ cucumber
4 tbsp sour cream (recipe on page 21)
2 tbsp dill tips

1| Dice the bread roll and soak in the milk for 10 minutes, then squeeze out well. Finely dice the bacon and fry in a pan over a medium heat until crispy. Put all the ingredients except the seasoning in a bowl, and combine well. Season to taste.

2| With damp hands, shape the mixture into 4 patties, then grill on each side for about 3–4 minutes. Halve the burger buns and toast the cut surfaces over the grill for a few moments.

3| To make the toppings, wash and shake dry the lettuce leaves. Trim, wash and slice the radishes. Peel and slice the cucumber.

4| Arrange the lettuce leaves on the bottom halves of the buns. Put 1 tablespoon of sour cream and one patty on each. Arrange the sliced radishes and cucumber on the burgers, and garnish with dill tips. Top with the remaining halves of the buns.

ORIENTAL BURGERS

FOR 4 PORTIONS
PREPARATION TIME: APPROX. 30 MINUTES

Per portion approx.:
624 kcal/2611 kJ
41 g P   37 g F   25 g CH

BUNS

1 pitta bread

PATTIES

1 stale bread roll
approx. 120 ml lukewarm milk
600 g minced beef
1 finely chopped onion
1 finely chopped garlic clove
2 eggs
2 tbsp freshly chopped parsley
½ tsp paprika powder
big pinch of cinnamon
salt
freshly ground pepper

TOPPINGS

200 g baby spinach leaves
1 pomegranate
100 g full-fat yoghurt
3 tbsp olive oil
salt
pepper

1| Dice the bread roll and soak in the milk for 10 minutes, then squeeze out well. Put all the ingredients except the seasoning in a bowl, and combine well. Season to taste.

2| With damp hands, shape the mixture into 4 patties, then grill on each side for about 3–4 minutes.

3| To make the toppings, wash and shake dry the spinach. Cut the pomegranate in half and scoop out the seeds, reserving the juice. Stir together the pomegranate seeds and juice, yoghurt and olive oil, and season with salt and pepper. Fold the spinach into the yoghurt and pomegranate dressing.

4| Cut the pitta bread into quarters. Slice each quarter in half and toast on the grill (or in an electric toaster). Put the patties and spinach on the bottom halves of the buns. Top with the remaining bread quarters and secure each portion with a wooden cocktail stick.

BURGERS WITH PEARS
AND GORGONZOLA

FOR 4 PORTIONS
PREPARATION TIME: APPROX. 30 MINUTES

Per portion approx.:
909 kcal/3803 kJ
53 g P   59 g F   43 g CH

BUNS

4 rye buns (recipe on page 15)

PATTIES

1 stale bread roll
approx. 120 ml lukewarm milk
600 g minced beef
1 finely chopped onion
2 eggs
½ tsp chilli powder
1 tsp dried rosemary
1 tsp dried oregano
salt
freshly ground pepper

TOPPINGS

100 g lamb's lettuce
1 large ripe pear
200 g Gorgonzola
4 tbsp crème fraîche
50 g chopped walnuts

1| Dice the bread roll and soak in the milk for 10 minutes, then squeeze out well. Put all the ingredients for the patties except the seasoning in a bowl, and combine well. Season to taste.

2| With damp hands, shape the mixture into 4 patties, then grill on each side for about 3-4 minutes. Halve the burger buns and toast the cut surfaces over the grill for a few moments.

3| To make the toppings, wash and shake dry the lettuce. Wash the pear and cut into quarters, cutting out the seeds. Cut each quarter into slices. Carefully slice the Gorgonzola cheese.

4| Spread each bottom half of the buns with 1 tablespoon of crème fraîche and place a lettuce leaf on top. Put a patty on each lettuce leaf. Arrange the Gorgonzola slices on the patty and the pear slices in a fan shape on top of the cheese. Sprinkle over the walnuts and serve with the top halves of the buns.

Goes with
BANANA AND ORANGE CHUTNEY

Per portion approx.:
95 kcal/397 kJ
1 g P   0 g F   21 g CH

2 oranges
2 ripe bananas
juice of 1 lime
1 red chilli pepper
honey

Squeeze the juice out of 1 orange. Cut the other one into segments and chop the orange segments into small pieces. Mash the bananas with a fork, and combine with the lime and orange juice. Deseed the chilli, then wash and chop finely and add to the chutney with the diced orange. Add a little honey according to taste.

WASABI BURGERS
DE LUXE

FOR 4 PORTIONS
PREPARATION TIME: APPROX. 35 MINUTES

Per portion approx.:
873 kcal/3653 kJ
49 g P   42 g F   60 g CH

BUNS

4 wheat buns (recipe on page 15)

PATTIES

1 stale bread roll
approx. 120 ml lukewarm milk
600 g minced beef
1 walnut-sized piece of ginger, freshly grated
2 tbsp finely chopped coriander leaves
big pinch of cinnamon
1 tsp ground cumin seed
2 eggs
salt
freshly ground pepper

TOPPINGS

4 large iceberg lettuce leaves
1 stalk lemon grass
400 g sugar snap peas
6 tsp mayonnaise (recipe on page 20)
2 tsp wasabi paste (hot green horseradish
    used in Japanese cooking)
2 tbsp sesame oil
2 tbsp soy sauce
pinch of sugar
freshly ground pepper

1| Dice the bread roll and soak in the milk for 10 minutes, then squeeze out well. Put all the ingredients for the patties except the seasoning in a bowl, and combine well. Then season to taste.

2| With damp hands, shape the mixture into 4 patties, then grill on each side for about 3-4 minutes.

3| To make the toppings, wash and shake dry the lettuce leaves. Wash the lemon grass and beat the lower, white part to soften in, then cut into thin slices and chop these finely. Wash and trim the sugar snaps. Stir together the mayonnaise and wasabi paste until well blended.

4| Heat the oil in a pan and sauté the lemon grass for about 2-3 minutes. Add the sugar snaps and cook over a high heat for just 1 minute, shaking the pan frequently. Add the soy sauce and season with sugar and pepper.

5| Brush each bottom half of the buns with 1 teaspoon of wasabi mayonnaise. Place a salad leaf and patty on each half. Arrange the sugar snaps on the meat, and top with the remaining halves of the buns.

ANDALUSIAN BURGERS

FOR 4 PORTIONS
PREPARATION TIME: APPROX. 30 MINUTES

Per portion approx.:
910 kcal/3808 kJ
64 g P   54 g F   48 g CH

BUNS

4 ciabatta buns (recipe on page 15)

PATTIES

1 stale bread roll
approx. 120 ml lukewarm milk
600 g minced beef
1 finely chopped onion
2 eggs
½ tsp habanero pepper paste
1 tsp dried oregano
1 tsp dried rosemary
salt
freshly ground pepper

TOPPINGS

2 red chilli peppers
75 g mayonnaise (recipe on page 20)
2 finely chopped garlic cloves
1 tbsp paprika powder
salt
8 slices serrano ham
8 slices manchego cheese
basil leaves to taste

1| Dice the bread roll and soak in the milk for 10 minutes, then squeeze out well. Put all the ingredients for the patties except the seasoning in a bowl, and combine well. Season to taste.

2| With damp hands, shape the mixture into 4 patties, then grill on each side for about 3-4 minutes. Halve the burger buns and toast the cut surfaces over the grill for a few moments.

3| To make the toppings, deseed the chillies, then wash and chop finely. Put in a mixer with the mayonnaise and garlic, and beat until smooth. Season with paprika powder and salt.

4| Spread the bottom halves of the buns with the paprika mayonnaise. Top each with 1 slice of ham and 1 of cheese, then 1 patty, and then 1 slice of cheese and 1 of ham. Add more paprika mayonnaise and basil leaves as desired, then top with the other halves of the buns.

Goes well with BBQ sauce (recipe on page 23).

Goes with
TOMATO AND CHILLI SALSA

Per portion approx.:
73 kcal/305 kJ
2 g P   3 g F   8 g CH

3 tomatoes
2 red onions
3 tbsp red wine vinegar
1 tbsp honey
1 tbsp rapeseed oil
1 tbsp chilli paste
2 tbsp freshly chopped coriander
    leaves
salt

Wash, deseed and finely chop the
tomatoes. Peel and finely chop the
onions. Stir together the vinegar,
honey, chilli paste and coriander.
Combine all the ingredients and
season with salt.

SURF & TURF

FOR 4 PORTIONS
PREPARATION TIME: APPROX. 35 MINUTES (PLUS MARINATING TIME)

Per portion approx.:
605 kcal/2531 kJ
46 g P   28 g F   41 g CH

BUNS

4 wheat buns (recipe on page 15)

PATTIES

4 beef fillet steaks (120 g each)
100 ml tomato juice
60 ml olive oil
2 dashes Tabasco
2 tbsp vodka
1 tbsp lemon juice
1 tsp zest of 1 unwaxed lemon
1 tsp cumin seeds
2 sprigs rosemary
4 garlic cloves
salt
freshly ground pepper

TOPPINGS

200 g ready-to-use (peeled and deveined)
    shrimps (heads removed)
1 red onion
4 tbsp mayonnaise (recipe on page 20)

1| Wash and pat dry the beef fillet. To make the marinade, stir together the tomato juice, 30 ml olive oil, Tabasco, vodka, lemon juice, 1 tablespoon lemon zest and the cumin seeds. Wash and shake dry the rosemary springs, then chop the needles. Stir half into the marinade. Peel and finely chop 2 of the garlic cloves, and also stir into the marinade.

2| Put the meat in a suitably sized freezer bag and pour in the marinade. Seal the bag well and leave the meat to marinate overnight.

3| 3 hours before cooking, put the shrimps, the remainder of the olive oil and lemon rind, the finely chopped garlic cloves and rosemary in a freezer bag and leave to marinate.

4| Put the meat and shrimps in a sieve and drain well, then pat dry. Season with salt and pepper and grill for about 6-8 minutes, turning two or three times. If you like, you can first thread the shrimps onto wooden sticks (soak the sticks first).

5| To make the toppings, peel and thinly slice the onion. Place some onion rings and 1 fillet on the bottom halves of the buns. Put 1 tablespoon of mayonnaise on each, and arrange the shrimps on top. Top with the other halves of the buns, and secure each bun with a wooden cocktail stick.

CAESAR'S SALAD BURGERS

FOR 4 PORTIONS
PREPARATION TIME: APPROX. 30 MINUTES

Per portion approx.:
726 kcal/3038 kJ
52 g P   40 g F   41 g CH

BUNS

4 wheat buns (recipe on page 15)

PATTIES

1 stale bread roll
approx. 120 ml lukewarm milk
600 g minced beef
1 finely chopped onion
2 eggs
1-2 tsp medium-hot mustard
1 tsp dried oregano
salt
freshly ground pepper

TOPPINGS

1 romaine lettuce
2 hard-boiled eggs
4 tbsp mayonnaise (recipe on page 20)
2 tbsp traditional soured cream
50 g grated Parmesan
salt
freshly ground pepper

1| Dice the bread roll and soak in the milk for 10 minutes, then squeeze out well. Put all the ingredients for the patties except the seasoning in a bowl, and combine well. Season to taste.

2| With damp hands, shape the mixture into 4 patties, then grill on each side for about 3-4 minutes. Halve the burger buns and toast the cut surfaces over the grill for a few moments.

3| To make the toppings, tear off the salad leaves, then wash them and shake them and slice into thin strips. Slice the eggs. In a small bowl, stir together the mayonnaise, soured cream and Parmesan, and season with salt and pepper.

4| Spread the bottom halves of the buns with the mayonnaise and layer with some of the shredded lettuce. Arrange the patties and more salad on top, and spread with more mayonnaise. Garnish with the slices of egg. Top with the remaining halves of the buns.

This burger is also delicious made with 1 thick slice of pastrami or corned beef instead of the patty.

PORK

Patties made of minced pork about 2 cm thick are grilled directly over a medium heat for about 3-4 minutes on each side. Just how long they will require is determined by the type of food, the barbecue or grill and the individually preferred level of doneness.

The meat goes well with spices and herbs such as cayenne pepper, curry, cloves, ginger, cardamom, coriander, bay leaves, marjoram or nutmeg.

BREAKFAST
BURGERS

FOR 4 PORTIONS
PREPARATION TIME: APPROX. 35 MINUTES

Per portion approx.:
1087 kcal/4548 kJ
63 g P   65 g F   54 g CH

BUNS

4 wheat buns (recipe on page 15)

PATTIES

1 stale bread roll
approx. 120 ml lukewarm milk
600 g minced pork
2 tbsp diced smoked bacon
10 g fried onions
2 eggs
20 g chopped green pepper (jar)
1 tbsp medium-hot mustard
1 tbsp chopped mild chilli
big pinch of chilli powder plus a little extra
    to garnish
salt
freshly ground pepper

TOPPINGS

4 slices of bacon
800 g baked beans
4 thick slices of cheddar
vegetable oil for frying
4 eggs

1| Dice the bread roll and soak in the milk for 10 minutes, then squeeze out well. Put all the other ingredients for the patties except the seasoning in a bowl, and combine well. Season to taste.

2| With damp hands, shape the mixture into 4 patties, then grill on each side for about 3–4 minutes. Halve the burger buns and toast the cut surfaces over the grill for a few moments.

3| To make the toppings, dry-fry the bacon in a pan until crispy, then remove and place on kitchen paper to drain. Heat the baked beans. Fry 4 eggs in a large pan with a little oil or butter.

4| Put 1 slice of bacon and 1 patty on each of the four bottom halves of the buns. Spoon generous helpings of baked beans over each. Place the cheddar on top, and finish with a fried egg. Dust with a little of the chilli powder and top with the remaining halves of the buns.

Goes with
MANGO AND CHILLI SALSA

◆━━━◆

Per portion approx.:
79 kcal/330 kJ
1 g P   1 g F   10 g CH

1 large ripe mango
1 red onion
½ a fresh red chilli pepper
2 tbsp oil
juice of 1 lime
salt
1 tsp brown sugar

◆━━━◆

Peel the mango, then cut the flesh
from the stone and chop into small
pieces. Peel and dice the onion.
Wash, deseed and finely chop the
chilli pepper. Combine all the ingredients with oil, lime juice, salt and
sugar, and leave to stand for about
20 minutes before serving.

CURRY BURGERS

FOR 4 PORTIONS
PREPARATION TIME: APPROX. 30 MINUTES

Per portion approx.:
703 kcal/2941 kJ
16 g P   44 g F   48 g CH

BUNS

4 wheat buns (recipe on page 15)

PATTIES

1 stale bread roll
approx. 120 ml lukewarm milk
600 g minced pork
1 walnut-sized piece of ginger, freshly grated
1 finely chopped onion
2 eggs
1-2 tsp curry powder
salt
freshly ground pepper

TOPPINGS

4 large green frisée lettuce leaves
1 red onion
4 tbsp mayonnaise (recipe on page 20)

1| Dice the bread roll and soak in the milk for 10 minutes, then squeeze out well. Put all the ingredients except the seasoning in a bowl, and combine well. Season to taste.

2| With damp hands, shape the mixture into 4 patties, then grill on each side for about 3-4 minutes. Halve the burger buns and toast the cut surfaces over the grill for a few moments.

3| To make the toppings, wash and shake dry the lettuce leaves. Peel and thinly slice the onion.

4| Spread 1 teaspoon of mayonnaise on each of the bottom halves of the buns. Place a lettuce leaf and patty on each. Divide the remainder of the mayonnaise and the onion rings among the burgers. Top with the remaining halves of the buns.

PARMA HAM BURGERS
WITH MOZZARELLA

FOR 4 PORTIONS
PREPARATION TIME: APPROX. 30 MINUTES

Per portion approx.:
1054 kcal/4410 kJ
76 g P   57 g F   41 g CH

BUNS

4 ciabatta buns (recipe on page 15)

PATTIES

1 stale bread roll
approx. 120 ml lukewarm milk
600 g minced pork
2 tbsp diced mild bacon
1 finely chopped onion
2 eggs
2 chopped firm small tomatoes
1 tbsp tomato paste
1 tbsp chopped curly-leafed parsley
1 tbsp pine kernels
1 tbsp balsamic vinegar plus a little extra
    to garnish
½ tsp paprika powder
sea salt
freshly ground pepper

TOPPINGS

150 g rocket
2 tbsp white balsamic vinegar
2 tbsp olive oil
salt
freshly ground pepper
12 slices Parma ham
300 g mozzarella affumicata (smoked)

1| Dice the bread roll and soak in the milk for 10 minutes, then squeeze out well. Put all the ingredients except the seasoning in a bowl, and combine well. Season to taste.

2| With damp hands, shape the mixture into 4 patties, then grill on each side for about 3-4 minutes.

3| To make the toppings, wash and shake dry the rocket, and shred any large leaves. Make a dressing from the balsamic vinegar, olive oil and the seasoning, and dress the salad. It shouldn't be too wet.

4| Halve the burger buns. Arrange the salad over the bottom halves and place the patty on top. Cut the mozzarella into thick slices and place on the patty. Loosely arrange 3 slices of the Parma ham over each. Drizzle over some balsamic vinegar, and season with a little salt and pepper. Top with the remaining halves of the buns.

Goes with
HAZELNUT PESTO

Per portion approx.:
330 kcal/1381 kJ
6 g P   13 g F   4 g CH

2 bunches flat-leafed parsley
8 large basil leaves
75 g hazelnuts
2 garlic cloves
60 ml olive oil
1 tbsp nut oil
3 tbsp grated Parmesan
salt
freshly ground pepper

Wash and shake dry the parsley and basil leaves. Blend with the hazelnuts and garlic cloves. Slowly add the oils, then stir in the Parmesan and check the seasoning. Drizzle generous quantities of the pesto over the mozzarella slices instead of the balsamic vinegar.

For a pesto verde:
Increase the quantity of herbs and omit the hazelnuts for a delicious pesto verde.

Goes with
GRILLED GREEN PEPPERS

Per portion approx.:
31 kcal/130 kJ
0 g P   3 g F   1 g CH
16 small green peppers (Pimientos
    de Padrón)
olive oil for drizzling
sea salt to sprinkle

Wash and trim the peppers, then drizzle with olive oil and grill until soft. Alternatively, fry the peppers in olive oil over a high heat, then cook for 4-6 minutes until they are soft. Sprinkle generously with sea salt before serving.

IBÉRICO BURGERS
WITH CHORIZO

FOR 4 PORTIONS
PREPARATION TIME: APPROX. 35 MINUTES

Per portion approx.:
1109 kcal/4640 kJ
60 g P   69 g F   45 g CH

BUNS

4 rye buns (recipe on page 15)

PATTIES

1 stale bread roll
approx. 120 ml lukewarm milk
600 g minced pork
2 tbsp diced smoked bacon
1 finely chopped red onion
1 finely chopped garlic clove
2 eggs
2 tbsp chopped red pepper
1 tbsp red paprika paste (Mojo)
big pinch of medium hot Pimentón de la
    Vera (Spanish smoked paprika powder)
sea salt
freshly ground pepper

TOPPINGS

200 g manchego
150 g chorizo
2 medium Kumato tomatoes
plenty of aioli (recipe on page 21) for
    spreading, garnishing and serving

1| Dice the bread roll and soak in the milk for 10 minutes, then squeeze out well. Put all the ingredients except the seasoning in a bowl, and combine well. Then season well to taste with the spices and seasoning.

2| With damp hands, shape the mixture into 4 patties, then grill on each side for about 3-4 minutes.

3| To make the toppings, thinly slice the manchego and cut the chorizo into very thin slices. Wash the tomatoes, cut out the stalks and slice them.

4| Halve the burger buns. Spread some of the aioli over the bottom halves. Arrange the manchego slices on top with the triangles protruding over the sides of the buns. Place the chorizo slices and patties on the cheese. Arrange the tomato slices on the patties and dollop on generous amounts of aioli. Top with the remaining halves of the buns. Serve with more aioli.

ALOHA BURGERS

FOR 4 PORTIONS
PREPARATION TIME: APPROX. 30 MINUTES

Per portion approx.:
928 kcal/3888 kJ
42 g P   58 g F   61 g CH

BUNS

4 wheat buns (recipe on page 15)

PATTIES

600 g pork fillet
salt
freshly ground pepper
2 tbsp forest honey
1 tbsp sesame seeds
4 slices semi-mature Gouda
red peppercorns

TOPPINGS

4 thick slices of pineapple
1 tbsp brown sugar
6 tbsp salad cream
1 small frisée lettuce
4 cocktail cherries

1| Cut the pork fillet diagonally into not-too-thick slices. Season the medallions well. Grill for no longer than 4-5 minutes on each side; the meat should still be tender and slightly pink on the inside. Brush lightly with forest honey while grilling. Sprinkle with sesame seeds after grilling, and place the cheese slices on the patties while they are still hot so the cheese melts. Sprinkle liberally with red peppercorns.

2| Sprinkle the pineapple slices with sugar, pressing down with a spatula if desired. Grill on each side for 2-3 minutes. The sugar should be lightly caramelised without letting the pineapple become soft.

3| Halve the burger buns, and spread the bottom halves with salad cream. Trim the lettuce. Wash and shake dry the leaves, then arrange on the buns with the pork medallions on top. Place the pineapple slices on top. Garnish with the whole, halved or thinly sliced cocktail cherries. Top with the remaining halves of the buns.

Goes with
APRICOT CHUTNEY

Per portion approx.:
928 kcal/3883 kJ
42 g P   42 g F   61 g CH

2 dried apricots
5 fresh apricots
1 tsp sunflower oil
pinch of dried cumin seeds
½ finely chopped red chilli pepper
1 tsp raisins
1 tsp freshly grated ginger
dash of lemon juice
salt
brown sugar

Thinly slice the dried apricots.
Then wash and pit the fresh apricots, and thinly slice the flesh. Heat
the sunflower oil in a saucepan and
add the dried cumin seeds. Put the
chopped chilli pepper, dried apri
cots, raisins and grated ginger in
the saucepan. Add the fresh apricots and 1 tablespoon of water.
Cook over a low heat until the
apricots are soft. Stir in the lemon
juice and season with salt and
brown sugar according to taste.
Leave until cool, then serve the
apricot chutney with the burgers.

BACON BURGERS
WITH PORCINI

FOR 4 PORTIONS
PREPARATION TIME: APPROX. 35 MINUTES (PLUS COOKING TIME)

Per portion approx.:
897 kcal/3753 kJ
49 g P   60 g F   40 g CH

BUNS

wheat buns (recipe on page 15)

PATTIES

1 stale bread roll
approx. 120 ml lukewarm milk
600 g minced pork
2 tbsp diced smoked bacon
2 finely chopped shallots
2 eggs
2 tbsp chopped dried porcini
1 tbsp grated Parmesan
4 thinly sliced sage leaves
salt
freshly ground pepper
4 slices of bacon

TOPPINGS

2 slices of bacon
250 g lamb's lettuce
600 g fresh porcini
vegetable oil for frying
20 g butter
1 tsp thyme leaves
½ finely chopped garlic clove
salt
freshly ground pepper
1 tbsp chopped parsley leaves
2 tbsp traditional soured cream

1| Dice the bread roll and soak in the milk for 10 minutes, then squeeze out well. Put all the ingredients except the seasoning in a bowl, and combine well. Season to taste.

2| With damp hands, shape the mixture into 4 patties, wrap the bacon slices around them and grill on each side for about 3-4 minutes. Halve the burger buns and toast the cut surfaces over the grill for a few moments.

3| To make the toppings, first fry the bacon in a pan until crispy. Remove from the pan and allow to cool a little, then crumble with your hands. Trim, wash and shake dry the lamb's lettuce.

4| Trim the porcini and cut into thick slices. Heat a little oil in a pan and fry the mushrooms. Add the butter, thyme and garlic and continue cooking. Season to taste and stir in the parsley and soured cream.

5| Arrange the lamb's lettuce over the bottom halves of the buns and drizzle with a little of bacon fat. Sprinkle the bacon over the salad and place the patties on top. Cover with the porcini and place the remaining halves of the buns on top.

Serve with BBQ sauce (recipe on page 23).

APPLE AND CHEESE
BURGERS

FOR 4 PORTIONS
PREPARATION TIME: APPROX. 30 MINUTES

Per portion approx.:
866 kcal/3623 kJ
52 g P   51 g F   51 g CH

BUNS

4 wheat buns (recipe on page 15)

PATTIES

1 stale bread roll
approx. 120 ml lukewarm milk
1 medium apple
600 g minced pork
1 finely chopped onion
2 eggs
1 tbsp hot mustard
1 tbsp chopped parsley leaves
salt
freshly ground pepper

TOPPINGS

4 slices of bacon
1 medium apple
1 red onion
4 tbsp sour cream (recipe on page 21)
4 slices semi-mature Gouda
punnet of cress

1| Dice the bread roll and soak in the milk for 10 minutes, then squeeze out well. Peel, core and finely chop the apple. Put all the ingredients except the seasoning in a bowl, and combine well. Season to taste.

2| With damp hands, shape the mixture into 4 patties, then grill on each side for about 3-4 minutes. Halve the burger buns and toast the cut surfaces over the grill for a few moments.

3| To make the toppings, fry the bacon in a pan over a medium heat until crispy. In the meantime, peel, core and quarter the apple, then slice the quarters. Remove the bacon from the pan, and quickly fry the apple slices in the hot fat. Peel and thinly slice the onion.

4| Spread the sour cream on the bottom halves of the buns. Place the patties, 1 slice of bacon and the onion and apple slices loosely on top. Put 1 slice of Gouda on top of each. Cut the cress off the stalks, then wash and dry and arrange over the cheese. Top with the remaining halves of the buns.

LAMB & GAME

Patties made of lamb or venison that are about 2 cm thick are grilled directly over a medium to high heat for about 4-5 minutes on each side. Of course the exact cooking time depends on the particular type of food, the barbecue or grill and your personal taste.

Lamb and venison are very strongly flavoured, so season them with strong herbs and spices such as lamb with mugwort, savoury, cloves, ginger, garlic, cumin, caraway, bay leaves, mint, thyme or lemon zest.

Venison is well suited to herbs and spices such as ginger, lemon, bay leaves, nutmeg, cloves, pimento, rosemary, thyme, juniper or cinnamon, and especially wild boar is also good with caraway.

GREEK LAMB BURGERS

FOR 4 PORTIONS
PREPARATION TIME: APPROX. 30 MINUTES

Per portion approx.:
768 kcal/3213 kJ
43 g P   39 g F   45 g CH

BUNS

4 wheat buns (recipe on page 15)

PATTIES

1 stale bread roll
approx. 120 ml lukewarm milk
1 garlic clove
1 shallot
600 g minced lamb
2 eggs
1 tsp dried oregano
salt
freshly ground pepper
100 g feta cheese

TOPPINGS

¼ iceberg lettuce
1 beef tomato
50 g black olives
50 g feta cheese
100 g Greek yoghurt
1 chopped garlic clove
salt
freshly ground pepper
smooth parsley leaves to garnish

1| Dice the bread roll and soak in the milk for 10 minutes, then squeeze out well. Crush the garlic. Peel and finely chop the shallot. Put all the ingredients for the patties except the spices and feta in a bowl, and combine well. Season the minced lamb to taste.

2| Cut the feta into four equally-sized pieces. With damp hands, shape the minced lamb into 4 spheres. Make a well in the middle of each. Put a piece of feta in each well, then seal it and shape the meat into patties. Grill the patties on each side for 4-5 minutes. Halve the burger buns and toast the cut surfaces over the grill for a few moments.

3| To make the toppings, wash the lettuce leaves and tear the leaves with your fingers. Slice the tomatoes and olives. Crush the feta with a fork and combine with the yoghurt and garlic. Season with salt and pepper.

4| Arrange some of the lettuce over the bottom halves of the buns. Place the patties, some more lettuce and more yoghurt dressing on top. Cover with the tomato slices, and garnish with olives and parsley. Top with the remaining halves of the buns, and secure each one with a cocktail stick.

PUMPKIN AND HALLOUMI
BURGERS

BUNS

4 ciabatta buns (recipe on page 15)

PATTIES

1 stale bread roll
approx. 120 ml lukewarm milk
600 g minced lamb
1 finely chopped shallot
2 eggs
½ courgette
100 g halloumi
1 garlic clove
½ tsp ground ginger
1 tsp dried thyme
salt and freshly ground pepper

TOPPINGS

120 g halloumi
1 finely chopped shallot
olive oil for frying
200 g pumpkin (e.g. Hokkaido,
    prepared weight)
100 ml vegetable stock
20 g butter
1 tsp thyme leaves
big pinch of cinnamon
½ tsp curry powder
freshly ground pepper
2 tbsp chopped pumpkin seeds
2 tbsp herb cream cheese

1| Dice the bread roll and soak in the milk for 10 minutes, then squeeze out well. Put in a bowl with the minced lamb, diced shallot and eggs, and combine well. Wash, trim and coarsely grate the courgette. Roughly chop the halloumi, then peel and crush the garlic. Work the courgette, cheese and garlic into the meat mixture. Season according to taste.

2| With damp hands, shape the mixture into 4 patties and grill on each side for about 4–5 minutes.

3| To make the toppings, first cut the halloumi in half lengthwise and grill on both sides until it colours slightly, but without it becoming tough. Wrap in aluminium foil to keep warm.

4| Fry the chopped shallot in a little oil in a large pan until glassy. Add the pumpkin flesh and cook for a few moments. Pour over the vegetable stock, and finish cooking. Bind with the butter. Stir in the thyme and seasoning, and check the flavour again. Dry-fry the pumpkin seeds in a pan.

5| Halve the ciabatta buns and spread with the cream cheese. Place the patties on top, and cover with plenty of cooked pumpkin. Cut the grilled halloumi into segments and arrange in a grid over the top. Sprinkle with pumpkin seeds, then place the remaining halves of the buns on top and secure each one with a cocktail stick.

Goes well with sweet potato wedges (recipe on page 17).

KEBAB BURGERS
WITH GRILLED VEGETABLES

FOR 4 PORTIONS
PREPARATION TIME: APPROX. 35 MINUTES (PLUS COOKING TIME)

Per portion approx.:
637 kcal/2665 kJ
44 g P   52 g F   51 g CH

BUNS

4 sesame wheat buns (recipe on page 15)

PATTIES

1 stale bread roll
approx. 120 ml lukewarm milk
400 g minced lamb
200 g minced beef
2 diced shallots
2 eggs
1 red chilli pepper
1 green chilli pepper
1 garlic clove
½ tsp sweet paprika powder
salt
freshly ground pepper

TOPPINGS

1 large red pepper
1 Spanish onion
1 aubergine
olive oil for drizzling
salt
20 g sugar
2 tbsp finely chopped mint leaves
100 g plain yoghurt
100 ml cream
freshly ground pepper

1| Dice the bread roll and soak in the milk for 10 minutes, then squeeze out well. Then place in a bowl with the minced beef, shallots and eggs, and combine well. Halve and deseed the chillies, then wash and chop finely. Peel and crush the garlic. Work everything into the meat mixture and season to taste.

2| With damp hands, shape the mixture into 4 patties and grill on each side for about 4–5 minutes.

3| To make the toppings, trim and wash or peel the vegetables, and cut into large segments or thick slices. Drizzle with olive oil and season, grill on both sides until the vegetables are soft and smell delightfully of roasting.

4| In a small saucepan, simmer the sugar, 1 tablespoon of mint leaves and 100 ml of water over a low heat. Stir frequently until the sugar has dissolved. Leave to cool, then whisk with the yoghurt and cream until creamy.

5| Halve the rolls and spread thinly with mint yoghurt. Arrange half the grilled vegetables over the buns. Place the patties on top, and cover them with the remainder of the vegetables. Grind some pepper over the top. Top with thick dollops of the mint yoghurt and sprinkle with the remainder of the mint leaves. Top with the other halves of the buns, and secure each bun with a wooden cocktail stick.

LAMB AND SPINACH
BURGERS

FOR 4 PORTIONS
PREPARATION TIME: APPROX. 35 MINUTES (PLUS STEAMING TIME)

Per portion approx.:
895 kcal/3745 kJ
57 g P   49 g F   53 g CH

BUNS

4 rye buns (recipe on page 15)

PATTIES

1 stale bread roll
approx. 120 ml lukewarm milk
10 black olives, pitted
600 g minced lamb
1 diced shallot
2 eggs
1 garlic clove
½ tsp ground cumin seed
1 tsp hot paprika powder
salt
freshly ground pepper

TOPPINGS

5 tsp mayonnaise (recipe on page 20)
3 tsp horseradish
500 g tender young spinach leaves
500 g leeks
2 tbsp butter
4 tbsp breadcrumbs
100 g freshly grated Parmesan
generous pinch of grated nutmeg
salt
freshly ground pepper
2 tbsp chopped flat-leafed parsley

1| To make the patties, dice the bread roll and soak in the milk for 10 minutes, then squeeze out well. Finely chop the olives. Put the minced lamb and the remainder of the ingredients (except for the seasoning and the garlic) in a bowl and combine well. Then peel and crush the garlic and work into the meat mixture. Season to taste.

2| With damp hands, shape the mixture into 4 patties, then grill on each side for about 4-5 minutes. Halve the buns, toast the cut surfaces over the grill for a few moments.

3| To make the toppings, stir together the mayonnaise and horseradish. Wash the spinach leaves and dry well. Wash and trim the leeks, then cut into thin slices.

4| Melt the butter in a pan and sauté the leeks over a medium heat for 8-10 minutes. Add the spinach and cook until slightly wilted. Remove from the hob. Drain the vegetables in a sieve if the mixture is too liquid. Combine the leeks, spinach, breadcrumbs and Parmesan in a bowl. Season to taste.

5| Brush the bottom halves of the buns with 1 teaspoon of horseradish mayonnaise. Arrange the spinach and leek mixture on the buns, and top each with 1 patty. Sprinkle over the chopped parsley. Brush equal amounts of the remaining mayonnaise on the tops of the buns, and place on the bottom halves.

Goes with
POMEGRANATE RELISH

Per portion approx.:
114 kcal/477 kJ
1 g P   7 g F   11 g CH

2 pomegranates
1 shallot
2 tbsp finely chopped basil leaves
1 tsp grated ginger
2 tbsp olive oil
4 tbsp cider vinegar
big pinch of cinnamon
big pinch of chilli powder
salt
freshly ground pepper

Halve the pomegranates and scoop out the seeds. Peel and finely chop the shallot. Combine the pomegranate seeds, diced shallot, basil and ginger in a bowl. Add the olive oil and cider vinegar, and season to taste. Leave to stand for about 30 minutes before serving.

LAMB AND AUBERGINE
BURGERS

FOR 4 PORTIONS
PREPARATION TIME: APPROX. 40 MINUTES (PLUS STANDING TIME)

Per portion approx.:
1229 kcal/5142 kJ
48 g P   93 g F   48 g CH

BUNS

4 wheat buns (recipe on page 15)

PATTIES

1 stale bread roll
approx. 120 ml lukewarm milk
1 onion
100 g feta cheese
600 g minced lamb
2 eggs
1 garlic clove
1 tsp dried sage
salt, freshly ground pepper

TOPPINGS

2 aubergines
salt, 2 beef tomatoes
1 sprig rosemary
4 tbsp olive oil
punnet of beetroot sprouts

For the salsa verde:
2 garlic cloves, 1 onion
1 tbsp pickled capers
2 tbsp sliced chives
2 tbsp chopped basil leaves
150 ml olive oil
½ tbsp raspberry vinegar
1 tbsp lime juice
salt and freshly ground pepper

1| Dice the bread roll and soak in the milk for 10 minutes, then squeeze out well. Peel and finely chop the onion, and cut the feta cheese into small cubes. Put the minced lamb and the remainder of the ingredients (except for the garlic and seasoning) in a bowl and combine well. Then peel and crush the garlic and work into the meat mixture. Season to taste. With damp hands, shape the mixture into 4 patties and grill on each side for about 4-5 minutes.

2| Wash and wipe dry the aubergines and cut into slices 1 cm thick. Sprinkle with a little salt, and leave for 5 minutes to draw out the juices.

3| In the meantime, to make the salsa verde, peel and finely chop the garlic and onion. Drain and finely chop the capers. Put the garlic, diced onion and capers in a bowl with the chives and basil. Add the oil, vinegar and lime juice, and combine well, season.

4| Slice the tomatoes, cutting out the stalks. Pat the aubergine slices dry with kitchen paper. Finely chop the rosemary and combine with the olive oil. Brush the aubergines with oil on both sides and season with salt. Grill on both sides for about 6-8 minutes until golden.

5| Halve the buns and brush half the salsa verde over the four bottom halves. Arrange the tomatoes over the buns. Place 1 patty on each, then arrange the aubergines on top, and cover the vegetables with the remainder of the salsa. Garnish with the sprouts, then place the remaining buns halves on top.

ARTICHOKE BURGERS

FOR 4 PORTIONS
PREPARATION TIME: APPROX. 30 MINUTES

Per portion approx.:
853 kcal/3569 kJ
46 g P   56 g F   43 g CH

BUNS

4 wheat buns (recipe on page 15)

PATTIES

1 stale bread roll
approx. 120 ml lukewarm milk
600 g minced lamb
40 g pine kernels
1 finely chopped shallot
2 eggs
2 tbsp chopped flat-leafed parsley
salt
freshly ground pepper

TOPPINGS

4 artichoke hearts (can)
100 g feta cheese
4 dried tomatoes in oil
1 tsp dried thyme
freshly ground pepper
4 tbsp crème fraîche
flat-leafed parsley stalks to garnish

1| Dice the bread roll and soak in the milk for 10 minutes, then squeeze out well. Put all the ingredients for the patties except the seasoning in a bowl, and combine well. Season to taste.

2| With damp hands, shape the mixture into 4 patties and grill on each side for about 4–5 minutes. Halve the burger buns and toast the cut surfaces over the grill for a few moments.

3| To make the toppings, drain the artichoke hearts and cut each one into 4 slices. Crush the feta with a fork. Drain and finely chop the tomatoes and combine with the feta. Stir a little of the tomato oil into the feta mixture, and season with thyme and pepper.

4| Spread each bottom half of the buns with 1 tablespoon of crème fraîche, and place the patties on top. Arrange the sliced artichokes over the patties. Spoon the tomato and feta mixture over the burgers. Top with the remaining halves of the buns.

VENISON BURGERS
WITH QUINCE AND CRANBERRY RELISH

FOR 4 PORTIONS
PREPARATION TIME: APPROX. 40 MINUTES (PLUS COOKING TIME)

Per portion approx.:
1046 kcal/4377 kJ
50 g P   25 g F   131 g CH

BUNS

4 rye buns (recipe on page 15)

PATTIES

600 g minced venison
3 finely chopped shallots
150 g diced unsmoked bacon
4 tbsp breadcrumbs, 2 eggs
1 teaspoon Dijon mustard
1 tsp chopped fresh thyme
1 tsp chopped fresh rosemary
1 teaspoon zest of 1 unwaxed orange
salt and freshly ground pepper

TOPPINGS

320 g quince (pear quince)
50 g brown sugar
250 ml sweet red wine (e.g. Marsala)
big pinch of cinnamon
cornflour to bind if desired

For the cranberry relish:
1 chilli pepper
2 large red onions, 1 pear
1 tbsp sunflower oil
50 ml white wine vinegar
juice of 1 orange
250 g cranberries (jar)
plus to sprinkle 100 g brown sugar
pinch of salt

1| Put the minced venison in a bowl and combine thoroughly with the remainder of the ingredients. Season with salt and pepper. With damp hands, shape the mixture into 4 patties and grill on each side for about 4-5 minutes. Halve the buns and toast the cut surfaces over the grill for a few moments.

2| To make the toppings, cut the quince in quarters, then peel them and cut out the cores, slice. Caramelise the sugar lightly in a pan, then pour over the wine. Simmer the quince until they start to turn soft and season with cinnamon. If necessary, add a little more wine and reduce. If desired, measure out 1 tablespoon of the liquid and combine with 1 tablespoon of cornflour. Pour over the quince and bind the liquid.

3| To make the relish, halve the chilli pepper and remove the seeds, then wash and chop into tiny pieces. Peel and finely chop the onions. Peel and quarter the pear, then cut out the cores and chop into chunks.

4| Heat the oil in a saucepan and sweat the chopped chilli and onions. Pour over the vinegar and orange juice, then fold in the cranberries, pear and sugar. Add a pinch of salt and simmer gently over a moderate heat until thickened. Leave to cool.

5| Spread the bottom halves of the buns generously with the cranberry relish. Place the patties on top, and arrange the quince slices over them. Drizzle with the wine reduction and scatter a few cranberries over it. Serve with the top halves of the buns.

POULTRY

Patties made of minced poultry about 2 cm thick are grilled directly over a medium to high heat for about 3-4 minutes on each side. Poultry is very tender, so the grilling time can sometimes be shorter than expected.

The meat harmonises well with herbs and spices such as mugwort, savory, tarragon, garlic, coriander, caraway, parsley, saffron, thyme and lemon grass.

CHICKEN BURGERS
WITH BACON

FOR 4 PORTIONS
PREPARATION TIME: APPROX. 25 MINUTES

Per portion approx.:
609 kcal/2548 kJ
41 g P   29 g F   45 g CH

BUNS

4 wheat buns (recipe on page 15)

PATTIES

600 g minced chicken (from your butcher)
1 chopped small onion
zest of 1 unwaxed lemon
2 tbsp traditional soured cream
1 egg
4 tbsp breadcrumbs
½ tsp curry powder
salt
freshly ground pepper

TOPPINGS

4 slices of bacon
4 large lettuce leaves
1 beef tomato
1 garlic clove
50 g mayonnaise (recipe on page 20)

1| Put all the ingredients except for the seasoning in a bowl and combine well, then season with salt and pepper according to taste.

2| With damp hands, shape the mixture into 4 patties and grill on each side for about 3-4 minutes. Halve the burger buns and toast the cut surfaces over the grill for a few moments.

3| To make the toppings, fry the bacon in a pan over a medium heat until crispy. In the meantime, wash and shake dry the salad. Wash the tomato and cut into 8 slices, discarding the stalk. Peel and finely chop the garlic. Stir the garlic into the mayonnaise.

4| Cover the bottom halves of the buns with lettuce and tomato slices. Place 1 patty and 1 slice of bacon on each bun, and finish with a generous dollop of the garlic mayonnaise. Finish with the top halves of the buns.

SESAME CHICKEN BURGERS
WITH ASPARAGUS

FOR 4 PORTIONS
PREPARATION TIME: APPROX. 40 MINUTES (PLUS COOKING TIME)

Per portion approx.:
873 kcal/3653 kJ
49 g P   54 g F   48 g CH

BUNS

4 sesame wheat buns (recipe on page 15)

PATTIES

600 g minced chicken (from your butcher)
1 chopped small onion
1 tsp zest of 1 unwaxed lemon
2 tbsp traditional soured cream
1 egg
4 tbsp breadcrumbs
1 tbsp sesame seeds
1 tbsp tahini (sesame paste)
salt
freshly ground pepper

TOPPINGS

150 g white asparagus
sugar, butter
½ a lollo bianco lettuce
4 slices prosciutto

For the hollandaise sauce:
1 unwaxed lemon
1 tsp white wine vinegar
½ tsp crushed white peppercorns
    plus a little more to sprinkle
2 egg yolks
120 g butter
salt

1| Put all the ingredients except for the seasoning in a bowl and combine well, then season to taste. With damp hands, shape the mixture into 4 patties and grill on each side for about 3-4 minutes. Halve the buns and toast the cut surfaces over the grill for a few moments.

2| Peel the asparagus. Cook in plenty of water with a pinch of sugar and the butter for about 10 minutes, making sure it doesn't get too soft. Cut into pieces 2-3 cm long and set aside. Wash and dry the lettuce.

3| To make the hollandaise sauce, start by halving the lemon. Heat the cut sides of the lemon on the grill for a few minutes. Squeeze one half and grate the rind.

4| Heat two tablespoons of water in a saucepan with the vinegar and peppercorns and reduce slightly, then leave to cool. Put the reduction in a metal bowl over hot water and whisk the egg yolks until foamy. Do not allow to boil! Melt the butter and slowly add to the egg mixture; whisk until thick. Season with salt, lemon juice and zest.

5| Spread the bottom halves of the buns thinly with the hollandaise sauce. Arrange the lettuce leaves on the buns. Drape the prosciutto over the lettuce. Put the patties on the ham, then the asparagus sections, and top them with dollops of the hollandaise sauce. You can also combine the asparagus and hollandaise sauce. Grate some pepper over the top and sprinkle with the remainder of the lemon zest. Top with the other halves of the buns. Serve with quarters of the roasted half lemon.

TANDOORI BURGERS
WITH CURRIED CAULIFLOWER

FOR 4 PORTIONS
PREPARATION TIME: APPROX. 30 MINUTES (PLUS COOKING TIME)

Per portion approx.:
970 kcal/4058 kJ
44 g P   49 g F   64 g CH

BUNS

4 naan breads with sesame seeds

PATTIES

600 g minced chicken (from your butcher)
1 chopped small onion
1 tsp lemon zest, 2 tbsp lassi
4 tbsp breadcrumbs, 2 tbsp dried prunes
1 egg, 1 tsp tandoori seasoning for chicken
big pinch of ground cardamom
1 tsp grated ginger
salt and freshly ground pepper

TOPPINGS

2 red peppers, 200 g cauliflower
200 g green beans (jar), 2 tbsp soy oil
1 finely chopped onion
2 tbsp red curry paste
150 ml coconut milk, 3 kaffir lime leaves
sugar, salt

For the curry sauce:
2 small ripe tomatoes, 2 tbsp vegetable oil
1 tsp mustard seeds, 2 tbsp chilli flakes
2 finely chopped onions
$\frac{1}{2}$ tsp ground coriander, $\frac{1}{2}$ tsp garam
    masala, $\frac{1}{2}$ tsp ground turmeric,
    $\frac{1}{2}$ tsp cayenne pepper
salt and freshly ground pepper
100 ml coconut milk

1| Put all the ingredients for the patties except for the seasoning in a bowl and combine well, then season to taste. With damp hands, shape the mixture into 4 burgers and grill on each side for about 3–4 minutes. Cut the naan breads in half and toast on the grill.

2| To make the toppings, trim, deseed and wash the peppers. Cut 1 of them into quarters, and the other into thin strips. Cook the quarters on the grill. Trim and wash the cauliflower and divide into florets. Halve the beans.

3| Heat the oil in a pan and fry the onion and curry paste. Pour over the coconut milk. Add the lime leaves and simmer to reduce, adding coconut milk if required. Take out the lime leaves and stir in the pepper strips and cauliflower. Simmer until the vegetables are soft, then stir in the beans. Season with sugar and salt.

4| To make the sauce, wash and quarter the tomatoes and cut out the stalks. Heat the oil in a pan and cook the mustard seeds until they burst open. Add the chilli flakes and onions and simmer until the onions are soft. Add the remainder of the spices and the tomatoes, and simmer for a further 5 minutes. Pour over the coconut milk, and simmer until you have a smooth, creamy sauce.

5| Spread one half of the bread with a little curry sauce, and cover with grilled pepper. Place 1 patty on the pepper. Heap the curried cauliflower over the patty and place the other half of the bread on top. Secure with cocktail sticks and serve with the remainder of the curry sauce.

ORANGE BURGERS
WITH CURRY AND GOAT'S CHEESE

FOR 4 PORTIONS
PREPARATION TIME: APPROX. 25 MINUTES

Per portion approx.:
744 kcal/3113 kJ
48 g P   36 g F   53 g CH

BUNS

4 rye buns (recipe on page 15)

PATTIES

600 g minced turkey (from your butcher)
1 chopped small onion
1 tsp zest of 1 unwaxed orange
2 tbsp traditional soured cream
1 egg
4 tbsp breadcrumbs
½ tsp curry powder
sea salt
freshly ground pepper

TOPPINGS

1 small lollo rosso lettuce
1 tbsp grapeseed oil
1 tbsp raspberry vinegar
sea salt
freshly ground pepper
1 large orange
2 tbsp forest honey
2 tbsp coarse-grained sweet mustard
4 small goat's cheeses (50 g each)

1| Put all the ingredients except for the seasoning in a bowl and combine well, then season to taste. With damp hands, shape the mixture into 4 patties and grill on each side for about 3–4 minutes. Halve the buns and toast the cut surfaces over the grill for a few moments.

2| To make the toppings, wash the lettuce and spin dry. Make a dressing out of the oil, vinegar, salt and pepper and marinate the salad, it should not get too wet.

3| Peel and fillet the orange. Warm the honey in a pan and coat the orange slices in it.

4| Spread the bottom halves of the buns with the mustard and cover loosely with the lettuce. Push the patties into the salad, and top with the goat's cheeses. Cover with the still-hot orange fillets, and drizzle over the honey from the pan. Top with the other halves of the buns and secure with wooden cocktail sticks.

TERIYAKI BURGERS

FOR 4 PORTIONS
PREPARATION TIME: APPROX. 35 MINUTES (PLUS MARINATING TIME)

Per portion approx.:
457 kcal/1913 kJ
38 g P   14 g F   40 g CH

BUNS

4 sesame wheat buns (recipe on page 15)

PATTIES

4 chicken breast fillets (125 g each)
4 tbsp soy sauce
2 tbsp sherry
1 tbsp grated ginger
1 finely chopped garlic clove
1 tsp honey

TOPPINGS

100 g rocket
1 beef tomato
1 onion
3 tbsp medium-hot mustard
1 tbsp honey
3 tbsp full-fat yoghurt
1 tbsp balsamic vinegar
2 tbsp olive oil
salt
freshly ground pepper

1| Wash and pat dry the chicken. Thoroughly combine the remainder of the ingredients for the marinade. Put the meat in a suitably sized freezer bag and pour in the marinade. Seal the bag well and leave the meat to marinate overnight.

2| Drain the chicken fillets and grill for 5-10 minutes on each side until they are done and golden. Halve the burger buns and toast the cut surfaces over the grill for a few moments.

3| To make the toppings, wash and dry the rocket. Wash and slice the tomato, cutting out the stalk. Peel and slice the onion.

4| Stir together the mustard, honey, yoghurt and balsamic vinegar, then add the oil and continue stirring until you have a creamy dressing. Season with salt and pepper.

5| Arrange some of the rocket over the bottom halves of the buns. Place the chicken fillets on top, then the sliced tomato, the remainder of the rocket and the onion rings. Drizzle over the honey and mustard dressing. Top with the other halves of the buns, and secure each one with a wooden cocktail stick.

PINEAPPLE BURGERS

FOR 4 PORTIONS
PREPARATION TIME: APPROX. 30 MINUTES

Per portion approx.:
714 kcal/2987 kJ
47 g P   34 g F   59 g CH

BUNS

4 ciabatta buns (recipe on page 15)

PATTIES

600 g minced chicken (from your butcher)
1 chopped small onion
2 tbsp traditional soured cream
1 egg
4 tbsp breadcrumbs
2 tbsp chopped flat-leafed parsley
1 tsp five-spice powder
salt
freshly ground pepper
4 slices fresh pineapple

TOPPINGS

4 large iceberg lettuce leaves
4 tsp mayonnaise (recipe on page 20)
1 tsp curry powder
big pinch of chilli powder
4 slices Gruyère

1| Put the minced meat with the other ingredients except the seasoning and pineapple in a bowl and combine well. Season to taste.

2| Wrap the meat mixture around the pineapple slices, avoiding the hole in the middle. Grill the patties on each side for 3–4 minutes. Halve the buns and toast the cut surfaces over the grill for a few moments.

3| In the meantime, to prepare the toppings wash the lettuce leaves and shake dry. Combine the mayonnaise, curry and chilli powder.

4| Spread each bottom half of ciabatta with 1 teaspoon of curry mayonnaise and place 1 lettuce leaf on top. Place the pineapple patty on the lettuce. Finish with 1 slice of cheese and the top half of the rolls.

MANGO AND CHICKEN
BURGERS

FOR 4 PORTIONS
PREPARATION TIME: APPROX. 30 MINUTES

Per portion approx.:
725 kcal/3033 kJ
44 g P   36 g F   59 g CH

BUNS

4 wheat buns (recipe on page 15)

PATTIES

600 g minced poultry (from your butcher)
1 chopped small onion
zest of 1 unwaxed lemon
2 tbsp traditional soured cream
1 egg
4 tbsp breadcrumbs
1 tsp pul biber (Turkish red pepper flakes)
salt
freshly ground pepper

TOPPINGS

1 ripe mango
1 radicchio
2 tbsp lime juice
1 tbsp honey
30 g meats of hazelnuts
100 g cream cheese
3 coriander stalks if liked

1| Put all the ingredients for the patties except for the seasoning in a bowl and combine well, then season with salt and pepper to taste.

2| With damp hands, shape the mixture into 4 patties and grill on each side for about 3-4 minutes. Halve the burger buns and toast the cut surfaces over the grill for a few moments.

3| To make the toppings, peel the mango, cut the flesh off the stone, and slice it into strips. Wash and spin dry the radicchio, then cut into thin slices. Stir together the lime juice and honey and combine with the radicchio. Roughly chop the hazelnuts.

4| Spread the bottom halves of the buns with cream cheese, and place the patties on top. Arrange the mango and radicchio on top and sprinkle over the hazelnuts. Garnish with coriander leaves if desired. Finish with the top halves of the buns.

FISH & SEAFOOD

Grill a whole fish over a low heat for about 10 minutes on each side, a fish fillet over direct medium heat for about 4-5 minutes on each side, and a patty made from minced meat (about 2 cm thick) over direct medium heat for about 2-3 minutes on each side. Seafood such as shrimp and prawns requires a total of about 2-5 minutes.

Flavour fish and seafood with basil, dill, tarragon, fennel, ginger, garlic, parsley, mustard or lemon.

TUNA BURGERS

FOR 4 PORTIONS
PREPARATION TIME: APPROX. 35 MINUTES

Per portion approx.:
613 kcal/2565 kJ
45 g P   27 g F   49 g CH

BUNS

4 wheat buns (recipe on page 15)

PATTIES

4 tuna steaks (150 g each)
juice of 1 lime
2 tbsp vegetable oil
salt
freshly ground pepper
1 tsp dried oregano

TOPPINGS

200 g pointed cabbage
1 small fennel bulb (approx. 200 g)
2 tbsp vegetable oil
1 tbsp white wine vinegar
1 tbsp honey
salt
freshly ground pepper
1 red chilli pepper
4 tsp ketchup (recipe on page 22)

1| Wash and pat dry the tuna steaks and sprinkle each side with lime juice. Combine the oil, salt, pepper and oregano and brush all over the fish. Grill carefully on both sides for about 2–4 minutes, taking care that the fish doesn't get too dry. Halve the buns and toast the cut surfaces over the grill for a few moments.

2| To make the toppings, trim, wash and dry the cabbage and cut into slices about 2 cm wide. Trim the fennel bulb, cutting out the stalk, root base, any brown areas and hard ribs. Reserve the leaves. Wash the bulb and slice crosswise into thin strips. Heat the oil in a pan and sauté the fennel strips for about 3 minutes. Add the cabbage and cook for a further 2 minutes. Add the vinegar and honey, and season with salt and pepper.

3| Wash, shake dry and finely chop the fennel leaves. Halve and deseed the chilli pepper, then wash and chop finely. Combine with the ketchup.

4| Spread the bottom halves of the buns with 1 teaspoon of chilli ketchup. Arrange the cabbage and fennel mixture over the top. Place 1 tuna steak on each and garnish with fennel leaves. Top with the other halves of the buns, and secure with wooden cocktail sticks.

Goes with
ROUILLE

Per portion approx.:
333 kcal/1393 kJ
12 g P   43 g F   10 g CH

1 yellow pepper
1 tbsp olive oil
2 slices dry baguette
1 fresh red chilli pepper
2 garlic cloves
salt
1 tbsp white wine
250 g mayonnaise
    (recipe on page 20)

First slice the pepper in half
lengthwise, then deseed, wash, dry
and dice. Heat the olive oil in a pan
and sauté the pepper for about
3 minutes. Cut the crusts off the
baguette and soak in water.
Afterwards squeeze out gently and
place in a bowl. Halve and deseed
the chilli pepper, then wash and
cut into thin slices. Peel and chop
the garlic cloves. Purée the pepper, chilli and garlic in a blender
with a little salt. Add the bread and
white wine and fold in. Stir this
creamy paste into the mayonnaise.
You can add a little more bread if
the mixture is too thin.

NY DELI BURGERS
WITH SHRIMPS

FOR 4 PORTIONS
PREPARATION TIME: APPROX. 30 MINUTES (PLUS STANDING TIME)

Per portion approx.:
397 kcal/1661 kJ
32 g P   17 g F   35 g CH

BUNS

4 rye buns (recipe on page 15)

PATTIES

juice of 1 lime
2 tbsp olive oil
salt
freshly ground pepper
1 garlic clove
2 sprigs of thyme
500 g prepared shrimps

TOPPINGS

200 g rocket
½ cucumber
zest of 1 unwaxed lime
1 tsp lime juice
4 tsp mayonnaise (recipe on page 20)
salt
pepper
2 stalks of chervil

1| Combine the lime juice, oil, salt and pepper in a large bowl to marinate the shrimps. Peel the garlic and crush into the marinade. Wash and shake dry the thyme and pluck off the leaves. Finely chop the thyme leaves and add to the marinade. Wash and pat dry the shrimps. Place in the marinade and leave for a short time.

2| In the meantime, wash and dry the rocket. Wash, peel and slice the cucumber. Combine the lime zest and juice with the mayonnaise.

3| Cook the shrimps on the grill for 2-4 minutes. Either thread the seafood onto wooden skewers or place them in an oiled grill dish. Reserve the remainder of the marinade. Halve the buns and toast the cut surfaces over the grill for a few moments.

4| Cover the bottom halves of the buns with 1 teaspoon of lime mayonnaise. Arrange the cucumber slices over the rolls and season with salt and pepper. Add the rocket and sprinkle over the remainder of the marinade. Arrange the shrimps over the salad. Wash and shake dry the chervil. Pluck the chervil leaves off the stalks and garnish the burgers with them. Top with the second halves of the buns.

Goes with
APPLE AND HORSERADISH DIP

❖

Per portion approx.:
131 kcal/548 kJ
2 g P   10 g F   9 g CH

1 small tart apple
2 tbsp lime juice
1 tbsp freshly grated horseradish
100 g plain yoghurt
100 g crème fraîche
1 tbsp chopped walnuts
1 tbsp finely chopped
    basil leaves
salt
freshly ground pepper

❖

Peel and core the apple, and grate to a pulp. Sprinkle over the lime juice immediately to prevent the apple from turning brown. Add the remainder of the ingredients apart from the seasoning. Combine well, and season to taste.

SALMON BURGERS
WITH SPINACH

FOR 4 PORTIONS
PREPARATION TIME: APPROX. 40 MINUTES

Per portion approx.:
780 kcal/3264 kJ
48 g P   35 g F   48 g CH

BUNS

4 wheat buns (recipe on page 15)

PATTIES

2 stale bread rolls
approx. 200 ml lukewarm milk
600 g salmon fillet
1 finely chopped onion
1 tbsp chopped curly-leafed parsley
1 tsp chopped tarragon leaves
1-2 eggs
grated potato if required
salt
freshly ground pepper
breadcrumbs

TOPPINGS

600 g baby spinach leaves
salt
1 garlic clove
100 g freshly grated Parmesan
big pinch of nutmeg
freshly ground pepper
4 sorrel leaves
4 tsp mayonnaise (recipe on page 20)

1| Dice the bread roll, soak in the milk and squeeze out well. Chop or thinly slice the salmon fillet. Put the roll and fish in a bowl with the other ingredients except for the seasoning and breadcrumbs, and combine well. Add a little water, another egg or a little grated potato and work in if the mixture is too dry. Season to taste.

2| With damp hands, shape the mixture into 4 patties and carefully coat in the breadcrumbs. Grill the patties on each side for about 2-4 minutes, turning carefully. Halve the buns and toast the cut surfaces over the grill for a few moments.

3| To make the toppings, pick over and wash the spinach. Blanche in a little salted water for 3-5 minutes. Drain, then squeeze out well. Peel the garlic and crush into the spinach. Add the Parmesan and combine well. Season with nutmeg, salt and pepper. Wash and shake dry the sorrel, then cut into thin strips.

4| Spread 1 teaspoon of mayonnaise over the bottoms of the buns. Arrange the spinach over the top. Place 1 patty on each bun and garnish with the sorrel strips. Top with the second halves of the buns.

FISH BURGERS
WITH DILL DRESSING

FOR 4 PORTIONS
PREPARATION TIME: APPROX. 35 MINUTES

Per portion approx.:
651 kcal/2724 kJ
42 g P   26 g F   51 g CH

BUNS

4 wheat buns (recipe on page 15)

PATTIES

2 stale bread rolls
approx. 200 ml lukewarm milk
600 g pollock fillet
1 finely chopped onion
1 tbsp chopped curly-leafed parsley
1 tsp chopped tarragon leaves
1-2 eggs
grated potato if required
salt
freshly ground pepper
breadcrumbs

TOPPINGS

punnet of watercress
½ cucumber
1 red onion
100 g light soured cream
2 tbsp chopped dill
dash of lemon juice
salt
freshly ground pepper

1| Dice the bread rolls and soak in the milk for 10 minutes, then squeeze out well. Mince the fish in a mincer or purée in a blender (not too finely). Put all the ingredients except the seasoning and the breadcrumbs in a bowl, and combine well. Add a little water, another egg or a little grated potato and work in if the mixture is too dry. Season to taste.

2| With damp hands, shape the mixture into 4 patties and gently coat in the breadcrumbs. Grill carefully on each side for about 3-4 minutes. Halve the burger buns and toast the cut surfaces over the grill for a few moments.

3| To make the toppings, trim the watercress, then wash, dry and chop. Peel and slice the cucumber. Peel and slice the onion. Combine the soured cream and dill, and season with lemon juice, salt and pepper.

4| Arrange a little of the watercress over the bottom halves of the buns and place the patties on top. Arrange the cucumber and onion slices on top, and finish with the watercress. Spoon the dill dressing over the top. Place the top halves of the buns on the watercress.

VEGGIES

We recommend cooking vegetarian patties (about 2 cm thick) over direct medium heat for about 3–4 minutes on each side, depending on the ingredients in your patties, of course.

———◆———

Basil, savoury, cayenne pepper, chilli, curry, tarragon, garlic, coriander, cumin, caraway, bay leaves, nutmeg, oregano, paprika, parsley and rosemary are just a few of the herbs and spices that will add the necessary flavour.

WILD GARLIC BURGERS

FOR 4 PORTIONS
PREPARATION TIME: APPROX. 35 MINUTES

Per portion approx.:
1033 kcal/4322 kJ
39 g P   80 g F   39 g CH

BUNS

4 wheat buns (recipe on page 15)

PATTIES

400 g halloumi
1 red chilli pepper
1 sprig rosemary
4 tbsp olive oil
1 tbsp lemon juice
2 garlic cloves
salt
freshly ground pepper

TOPPINGS

1 aubergine
1 courgette
2 red onions

For the wild garlic pesto:
bunch of wild garlic
50 g ground almonds
50 g freshly grated Parmesan
100 ml olive oil
salt
freshly ground pepper

1| To make the pesto, wash the wild garlic, then shake dry and cut into thin strips. Dry-fry the almonds in a small pan. Purée the wild garlic, almonds, olive oil and Parmesan in a mortar and pestle. Alternatively, you can purée them in a blender. Season with salt and pepper.

2| Cut the halloumi in half lengthwise. Slit open and deseed the chilli, then wash and finely chop. Wash and shake dry the rosemary, and chop the needles. Combine the chilli, rosemary and oil, then stir in the lemon juice. Peel the garlic cloves and crush into the marinade. Season with salt and pepper.

3| To make the toppings, wash and wipe dry the aubergine and courgette, then trim and cut into slices. Peel and thinly slice the onions.

4| Brush half the marinade over both sides of the halloumi slices. Use the remaining half for the avocado and courgette slices. Place the cheese and vegetables on the grill, cook on both sides for 4–6 minutes until brown.

5| Halve the buns and brush half the wild garlic pesto over the bottom halves. Arrange the aubergine and courgette slices over them. Place 1 slice of halloumi on each, drizzle over the remainder of the pesto, garnish with the onion rings. Top with the other halves of the buns.

VEGGIE BURGERS
WITH HERB DIP

FOR 4 PORTIONS
PREPARATION TIME: APPROX. 30 MINUTES (PLUS SOAKING TIME)

Per portion approx.:
416 kcal/1741 kJ
21 g P   13 g F   92 g CH

BUNS

4 rye buns (recipe on page 15)

PATTIES

1 tbsp oil
1 finely chopped onion
150 g green spelt
vegetable stock for soaking
1 carrot
2 tbsp chopped parsley
1-2 eggs
grated potato if required
salt
freshly ground pepper

TOPPINGS

4 large lettuce leaves
2 tomatoes
½ bunch radishes
1 red onion
4 tbsp ketchup (recipe on page 22)

1| Heat the oil in a pan and fry the onions until glassy. Add the spelt and vegetable stock. Leave the spelt to absorb the liquid for about 10 minutes, then cool. Meanwhile, trim, peel and finely grate the carrot. Add the carrot, parsley and 1 egg to the cooled spelt and combine well. Add a little water, another egg or a little grated potato and work in if the mixture is too dry. Season to taste.

2| With damp hands, shape the mixture into 4 patties and grill on each side for about 6 minutes.

3| To make the toppings, wash and shake dry the lettuce leaves. Wash, trim and slice the tomatoes and radishes. Peel and slice the onion.

4| Spread the bottom halves of the buns with ketchup and arrange the lettuce leaves on top. Arrange the patties and the slices tomatoes, radishes and onion on the buns. Top with the other halves of the buns, and secure each one with a wooden cocktail stick.

VEGGIE BURGERS
WITH POINTED CABBAGE

FOR 4 PORTIONS
PREPARATION TIME: APPROX. 30 MINUTES (PLUS SOAKING TIME)

Per portion approx.:
503 kcal/2105 kJ
18 g P   18 g F   67 g CH

BUNS

4 wheat buns (recipe on page 15)

PATTIES

150 g bulgur wheat
vegetable stock for soaking
1 medium carrot
1 finely chopped onion
1 garlic clove
1 tbsp flour
4 tbsp breadcrumbs
1 tbsp chopped flat-leafed parsley
1–2 eggs
grated potato if required
1 tsp ground coriander
salt
freshly ground pepper

TOPPINGS

50 g sesame seeds
150 g pointed cabbage
1 carrot
2 tbsp rice vinegar
1 tbsp sesame oil
salt
freshly ground pepper
½ cucumber
4 tbsp ketchup (recipe on page 22)

1| Soak the bulgur wheat in stock in accordance with the packet instructions. Trim, peel and finely grate the carrot. Put the bulgur, slightly cooled, in a bowl with the carrot and chopped onion. Peel the garlic and crush over it. Add the flour, breadcrumbs, parsley and whisked egg, and knead. Add a little water, another egg or a little grated potato and work in if the mixture is too dry. Season to taste.

2| With damp hands, shape the mixture into 4 patties and grill on each side for about 4–5 minutes. Halve the burger buns and toast the cut surfaces over the grill for a few moments.

3| To make the toppings, dry-fry the sesame seeds in a pan. Trim and wash the cabbage, then dry and cut into thin slices. Peel and grate the carrot. Make a dressing with the vinegar, oil, salt and pepper, and stir into the cabbage and carrot. Fold the sesame seeds into the salad. Peel and slice the cucumber.

4| Spread ketchup over the bottom halves of the buns. Place the patties on top, and arrange the sliced cucumber and cabbage over them. Top with the remaining halves of the buns.

CHICKPEA BURGERS
WITH BEAN AND CHILLI SALSA

FOR 4 PORTIONS
PREPARATION TIME: APPROX. 35 MINUTES (PLUS COOKING TIME)

Per portion approx.:
912 kcal/3816 kJ
36 g P   22 g F   143 g CH

BUNS

1 pitta bread with sesame

PATTIES

1 tbsp vegetable oil
1 finely chopped garlic clove
1 finely chopped shallot
1 green chilli, deseeded and finely chopped
big pinch of garam masala
big pinch of ground turmeric
1 tsp ground cumin seed
500 ml vegetable stock
250 g pumpkin (prepared weight)
200 g chickpeas (can)
2 tbsp roasted chickpea flour
handful of roughly chopped coriander
2 tbsp breadcrumbs, sea salt

TOPPINGS

2 tbsp olive oil
1 finely chopped onion
2 finely chopped garlic cloves
1 red pepper, deseeded and finely chopped
1 can kidney beans (approx. 400 g)
1 can chopped tomatoes (approx. 400 g)
2 tbsp roughly chopped coriander leaves
2 tbsp cumin seeds
1 tbsp ground chilli plus a little extra for
    sprinkling
2 peeled beetroot
4 tbsp traditional soured cream

1| Heat the oil in a pan and sauté the garlic, diced shallot and chilli until soft. Add the garam masala, turmeric and cumin, and cook for a few seconds, set aside.

2| Bring the vegetable stock to the boil. Dice the pumpkin and cook in the stock, then add the chickpeas and cook for a few more minutes. Drain and blend, but not too finely. Add the flour, coriander, breadcrumbs and the contents of the pan. Combine thoroughly, then check the seasoning.

3| With moist hands, shape into patties, using a little more breadcrumbs if necessary, then grill carefully for 2-3 minutes on both sides. Cut the pitta bread into quarters, then open out the quarters and toast on the grill.

4| For the toppings, heat the olive oil in a pan, and sauté the onion, garlic and pepper until soft. Add the beans, tomatoes and seasoning, and simmer until smooth and velvety. Add a little water if required, mash lightly, season well. Cut the beetroot into very thin slices.

5| Spread the bean and chilli salsa generously over the bottom halves of the pitta bread, and put the patties on top. Cover with the sliced beetroot and spoon a large dollop of soured cream on top. Sprinkle with chilli powder. Top with the remaining pieces of bread.

Goes well with nachos (recipe on page 17).

Goes with
TOMATO AND CORIANDER DIP

Per portion approx.:
47 kcal/197 kJ
1 g P   3 g F   3 g CH

4 tomatoes
10 coriander stalks
1 finely chopped onion
2 finely chopped
    garlic cloves
1 tbsp sesame oil
salt
freshly ground pepper

Pour boiling water over the tomatoes, then skin, deseed and chop
into small pieces. Pull the leaves off
the coriander stalks and chop
finely. Combine the tomatoes, coriander, chopped tomato and garlic,
and pour over the sesame oil.
Season with salt and pepper.

ASIAN
LENTIL BURGERS

FOR 4 PORTIONS
PREPARATION TIME: APPROX. 35 MINUTES (PLUS COOKING TIME)

Per portion approx.:
376 kcal/1573 kJ
17 g P   14 g F   54 g CH

BUNS

4 wheat buns (recipe on page 15)

PATTIES

300 g red lentils
1 tbsp oil
1 finely chopped onion
1-2 eggs
1 tsp freshly grated ginger
1 tsp cumin seeds
salt
freshly ground pepper
30-50 g wheat bran
grated potato if required

TOPPINGS

1 romaine lettuce heart
2 spring onions
½ red chilli pepper
2 tbsp lime juice
2 tbsp soy sauce
½ cucumber
coriander leaves for garnishing

1| Cook the lentils in accordance with the packet instructions, then drain and leave to cool. Heat the oil in a small pan and sauté the chopped onion until soft, then add to the lentils with 1 egg and the seasoning. Slowly add the wheat bran to the lentils until the mixture is firm enough to shape patties. Add a little water, another egg or a little grated potato and work in it the mixture is too dry. Check the seasoning, and add more if required.

2| With damp hands, shape the mixture into 4 patties and carefully grill on each side for about 4-5 minutes. Halve the burger buns and toast the cut surfaces over the grill for a few moments.

3| To make the toppings, trim, wash and dry the romaine lettuce and cut into strips. Trim and wash the spring onions, and cut the white sections into thin rings. Deseed and wash the chilli pepper and chop into small pieces. Combine the lime juice and soy sauce, and combine with the other ingredients apart from the cucumber and coriander. Peel and slice the cucumber.

4| Arrange the sliced cucumber on the bottom halves of the buns and place the patties on top. Loosely place more cucumber slices and the salad on top of the patties. Garnish with coriander leaves. Top with the remaining halves of the buns.

PEANUT BUTTER BURGERS

Per portion approx.:
481 kcal/2013 kJ
19 g P   18 g F   61 g CH

BUNS

4 rye buns (recipe on page 15)

PATTIES

150 g bulgur wheat
vegetable stock for soaking
1 onion
2 tbsp butter
200 g peas (jar)
salt
pinch of sugar
1 tbsp flour
4 tbsp breadcrumbs
1 tbsp chopped flat-leafed parsley
1–2 eggs
grated potato if required
freshly ground pepper

TOPPINGS

400 g rocket
1 large beef tomato
1 tbsp olive oil
1 tsp raspberry vinegar
salt
freshly ground pepper
4 tbsp crunchy peanut butter

1| Soak the bulgur wheat in stock in accordance with the packet instructions. Peel and finely chop the onion. Melt the butter in a saucepan, sauté the onion until glassy. Stir in the peas, salt and sugar. Pour over a little water and simmer for about 10 minutes. Drain the water.

2| Combine the bulgur, peas, flour, breadcrumbs, parsley and beaten egg in a bowl. Add a little water, another egg or a little grated potato and work in if the mixture is too dry. Season to taste.

3| With damp hands, shape the mixture into 4 patties and brown on the grill for about 10 minutes, turning carefully. Halve the buns and toast the cut surfaces over the grill for a few moments.

4| For the toppings, wash, dry and finely chop the rocket. Wash and slice the tomato, cut out the stalk. Make a light dressing with the oil, vinegar and seasoning.

5| Spread the bottom halves of the buns with peanut butter and arrange the rocket leaves on top. Drizzle a little dressing over the salad. Place the patties on top, and arrange the tomato slices over them. Top with the remaining halves of the buns.

ROQUEFORT BURGERS

FOR 4 PORTIONS
PREPARATION TIME: APPROX. 30 MINUTES (PLUS SOAKING AND COOKING TIME)

Per portion approx.:
734 kcal/3071 kJ
29 g P   43 g F   55 g CH

BUNS

4 rye buns (recipe on page 15)

PATTIES

30 g dried soy beans
1 red onion
1 medium carrot
80 g Roquefort
60 g ground almonds
1 tbsp chickpea flour
4 tbsp breadcrumbs
1 tbsp sesame seeds
1 egg
1 tsp ground cumin seed
1 tsp soy sauce
1 tsp ground coriander
salt
freshly ground pepper
2 tbsp olive oil

TOPPINGS

4 frisée lettuce leaves
2 pears
150 g Roquefort
100 g plain yoghurt
2 tbsp crème fraîche
1 tsp lemon juice
salt
freshly ground pepper

1| Soak the soy beans in cold water for 24 hours, then rinse and drain well. Alternatively, you can also use canned soy beans (approx. 100 g), which do not require soaking or cooking.

2| Put the beans in a large saucepan and cover with water, then simmer over a low heat for about 1 hour 30 minutes until soft. Pour off the water, then rinse the beans and leave to drain.

3| Peel and finely chop the onion, and trim, peel and finely grate the carrot. Roughly chop the beans, onion, carrot, cheese and almonds in a blender. Combine in a bowl with all the other ingredients except the seasoning and olive oil. Season to taste.

4| With moist hands, shape the mixture into 4 patties. Brush on both sides with the olive oil and brown on the grill for about 10 minutes, turning carefully. Halve the buns and toast the cut surfaces over the grill for a few moments.

5| To make the toppings, wash and shake dry the lettuce leaves. Peel and quarter the pears, then cut out the cores and slice the flesh. Crush the cheese with a fork, and combine with the yoghurt, crème fraîche and lemon juice. Season to taste.

6| Put 1 lettuce leaf on each bottom half of a bun. Place the patties on top and garnish with the pear slices. Spread over the Roquefort cream. Place the top halves of the buns on top, and secure with small wooden skewers.

RECIPE INDEX

Aioli 21
Aloha burgers 64
Andalusian burgers 48
Apple and cheese burgers 68
Apple and horseradish dip 108
Apricot chutney 65
Artichoke burgers 83
Asian lentil burgers 123

Bacon burgers with porcini 67
Banana and orange chutney 46
BBQ sauce 23
Breakfast burgers 56
Buffalo ranch burgers 30
Burgers with bacon and
    radishes 40
Burgers with pears and
    Gorgonzola 44

Caesar's salad 18
Caesar's salad burgers 52
Chanterelle burgers 39
Chicken burgers with bacon 88
Chickpea burgers with bean
    and chilli salsa 121
Ciabatta buns 15
Cole slaw 19
Corn on the cob 28
Curry burgers 59

Deep-fried onion rings 19
Double-double cheeseburgers 29

Fish burgers with dill dressing 110

Greek lamb burgers 73
Grilled green peppers 62
Guacamole 22

Hamburgers 26
Hazelnut pesto 61
Herb dip 116
Home-made fries 16
Hot cheese dip 125
Hot hamburgers 33

Ibérico burgers with chorizo 63

Kebab burgers with grilled
    vegetables 77
Ketchup 22

Lamb and aubergine burgers 81
Lamb and spinach burgers 78

Mango and chicken burgers 101
Mango and chilli salsa 58
Marsala mushrooms 31
Mayonnaise 20
Mediterranean burgers 35
Mexican burgers 36

Nachos 17
NY Deli burgers with shrimps 107

Orange burgers with curry
    and goat's cheese 95
Oriental burgers 42

Paprika relish 34
Parma ham burgers with
    mozzarella 60

Peanut butter burgers 124
Pesto verde 61
Pineapple burgers 98
Pomegranate relish 79
Pumpkin and halloumi
    burgers 74

Roquefort burgers 127
Rouille 106
Rye buns 15

Salmon burgers with spinach 109
Sesame chicken burgers with
    asparagus 91
Sour cream 21
Surf & turf 51

Tandoori burgers with curried
    cauliflower 92
Teriyaki burgers 97
Tomato and chilli salsa 50
Tomato and coriander dip 122
Tuna burgers 104

Veggie burgers with herb dip 117
Veggie burgers with pointed
    cabbage 118
Venison burgers with quince
    and cranberry relish 84

Wasabi burgers de luxe 47
Wedges 17
Wheat buns 15
Wild garden herb salad 19
Wild garlic burgers 114